One Room
at a Time •
THE BATHROOM

Your Essential Guide to a Beautiful Eco-Conscious Healthy-Living Lifestyle

Release

Revitalize

Renew

Charisse Marei

Mariana...
Enjoy the journey & lifestyle to live a healthy lifestyle with love & clarity, Balance + Purpose

Luv...
Mariane

I am conscious of
my thoughts
and the passion
and the desire
that manifest my creations.

Introduction

ENTER .....

Contents

Introduction
ENTER

1
The Bathroom
PURPOSE

2
Out with the Old
RELEASE

3
In with the New
RENEW

4
Clearing the Clutter
REVITALIZE

5
Yin and Yang of Organization
HARMONY

6
Breathe-able Eco-Cleaning
JOY

7
Eco-Conscious Design
PASSION

8
Water Consciousness
AWARENESS

9
A Treasure Chest of Well-Being
MANIFEST

10
PP Eco-Resources
LOVE

Acknowledgments

About the Author

To My Parents, Brothers, and Sisters

As I reflect on daily childhood memories about family, I realize I would never trade those times.
I never thought about those days ending and another phase beginning.
I never thought to think.
I think now.
I reflect now.

Oh

How I wish to recapture the busyness, the laughter, the standing in line.
The pajamas, the curlers, the uniforms, the play clothes, the robes and slippers.
Calling for each other, sharing secrets, laughing, crying.
Those days came to an end, unexpectedly, one by one, as each of us moved out.
Tears now flood my eyes; how sad.
How did it feel, Mom and Dad, when each of us left to begin a new leg of our journey?
The lines grew smaller.
The time grew longer.
The bathroom
remained
the
same.

With sparkle in my heart,
I dedicate this book to my hubby, Dr. Drew, and
"The Girls," Sage and Citrus.
Love you with every breath.

It all begins with the planting of a seed • • •

Treasure Your Book

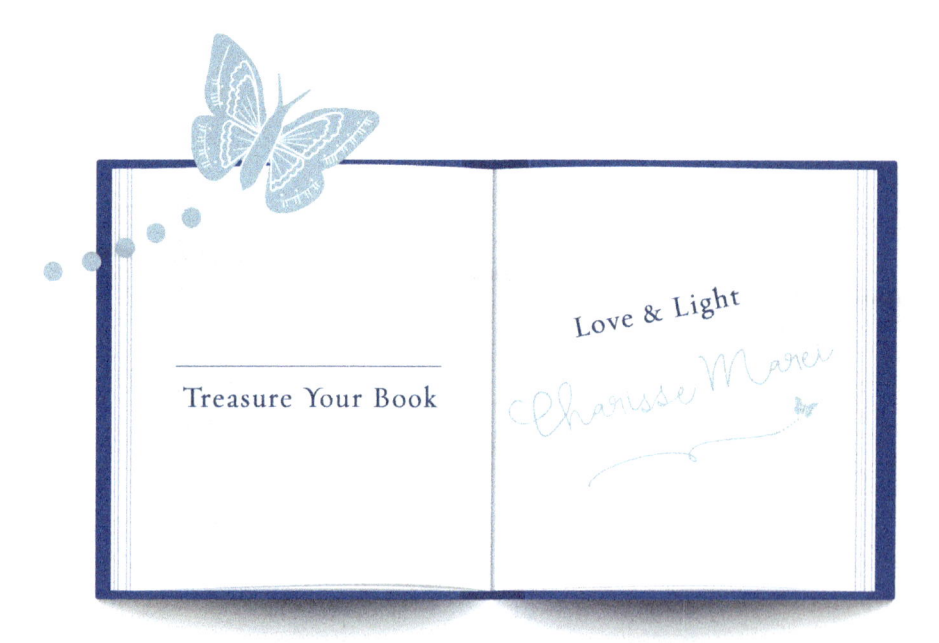

Love & Light
Charisse Maree

Welcome to a Small Slice of My World!

My book series, One Room at a Time, started with a single thought. My thought.

It began early one morning with seven splashes of cold water over my face, then a reach for my toothbrush. The circular motion of toothbrush bristles required water. As I watched the water swirl down the drain, I wondered how much water was wasted while performing my morning routine. I consciously conserve water. Does everyone follow this practice?

With toothbrush still in hand, I looked up at the mirror. As my eyes shifted, each blink captured a quick snapshot of compositions behind me. Sitting atop the pearlized golden glass tile on the bathtub surround were three shimmering round hatboxes that formed a three-tiered structure. The top box showcased six rolled, white voguish bath towels branching up and outward like flowers on a stem.

The toilet room door, slightly ajar, exposed a glimpse of illumination radiating from the Tuscan pendant light fixture enveloped in intricate gold filigree artwork and accented with pale-cream scavo glass. A fluffy white, tone-on-tone cotton bath mat was positioned just outside the shower door, ready to absorb the drips from ten sopping toes. The nine-inch-tall freestanding mermaid mirror perched atop a quirky chest of mini glass drawers granted a subtle passing glance. Each mental snapshot became an inspiration for this first book in the series: *The Bathroom*.

I reminisced about various stages of pulling this bathroom all together. I embraced my intentions and created selections that led to the final design. You see, there is so much more than what meets the eye. The overall design process involved being conscious of what I breathe, touch, and hear, how I feel, and why I freely enter the bathroom to Release, Renew, Revitalize (3Rs).

It did not stop there, for once the final touches were in place, the need to maintain balance and harmony became essential. Daily, weekly, monthly, and semi-annual rhythmic rituals were part of the plan. These were the necessary ingredients to surround myself in an environment that continually supports a fulfilling journey to a beautiful Eco-Conscious, Healthy-Living Lifestyle.

As I stood leaning against the vanity, creative ideas began to flow freely. I imagined writing a book to guide others beyond my circle of immediate influence. The desire tugged at my heart and strengthened with time. My thoughts began to appear as my pencil glided across the paper, forming one word at a time. Excitement stirred!

I have begun an interactive book series to help you achieve a unifying, Eco-Conscious Lifestyle—though simply One Room at a Time.

We begin with *The Bathroom*, for this is where we begin and end each day, every day.

Keep it simple. Keep it organized. Keep it eco-friendly.

A Necessity

As you hold this book in your hands, I ask, where do you reside? Are you in the Northern or Southern Hemisphere? What continent? Do you own a home or rent? Do you reside in a London townhouse, a Paris apartment, a villa in the islands, a single home in the suburbs, a row home in the city, or a flat?

Is your home 25,000 square feet, 225 square feet, or somewhere in between? Do you live on a boat or in a hotel? How many bathrooms and powder rooms? Per floor? While traveling by boat, plane, or train, is there a restroom? While on holiday, shopping, dining, and entertaining, are there restrooms?

Of course.

How many times throughout the day do you utilize the bathroom? For yourself, to help a loved one or child, or to wash the paws of your furry friends?

Countless.

We excuse ourselves to visit the bathroom, half bath, restroom, washroom. We visit to Release, Renew, Revitalize—to make ourselves prim and proper, to tidy up, to remove a mishap, to make little touch-ups, to wash up, to chitchat, to stay connected through social media, to help a friend, or to prepare for a special occasion.

Essentially, this special space is a universal room on a grand scale yet quite personal on an individual small scale. Today, I invite you to narrow in and focus on your personal bathroom or half bath.

It's all about you!

You walk to and into the bathroom upon rising each morning. In the evening before retiring, you repeat the steps in reverse. Repetition is key. It's how you live out the repetition that matters.

From my writing desk to your home, near or far, I believe you agree, the bathroom is one of your closest friends.

The bathroom is a necessity.

The Purpose

The purpose of the bathroom should not be understated. The bathroom is quite special. Our day, every day, begins and ends in this special place. You begin with sleepy eyes capturing a quick glance in the mirror, and end with a flip of the switch as you methodically exit before climbing into your comfy bed.

The purpose of creating *The Bathroom* book is simple. You see, an awe-inspiring bright light shines within each of us to guide us along an inspiring journey of transformation. An Eco-Conscious, Healthy-Living Lifestyle is a reflection of this light that provides nourishment from the inside out and the outside in—so you can live a life you have only dreamed of living. Age is not a factor!

Greatest Generation
Silent Generation
Baby Boomer
Gen X
Gen Y (Millenials)
Gen Z
Gen Alpha

My Gift

My gift to you is a timeless treasure chest of information all wrapped up into a specially designed series called One Room at a Time. They are your personal traveling companions. Pop them into the ChaCha bag (page 12) and take on a flight, or carry to the beach, take it on vacation, to a design store, or to a friend's home. Bring your books to a cafe and gather information while enjoying a cup of tea or a hot bowl of soup. Feel the energy. Make them your own.

Each book in the series is designed as your personal guide toward a beautiful Eco-Conscious, Healthy-Living Lifestyle. Enjoy the whimsical flair along this personal, informative, interactive, and inspiring journey you're about to take.

Each book also contains its own interactive workbook to guide you along an action-inspiring path. It's the one place to store and record information for present and future needs. Inspirations, recipes, how-to's, to-do's, happy eco-shopping lists, and much more are designed with you in mind. Take ownership of your book. Personalize it.

The entire series also involves *A Timeless Keepsake*, a journal designed to record personal story journeys. Fill the journal with treasures while reflecting on questions about personal life experiences, for you hold the map to treasures from years gone by, the present, and what is yet to come. Be aware. Be ready . . .

You may laugh, you may cry.
You may embrace, you may share.
It's your journey.

Write your story as you see it. As you feel it. You do not need a degree or a certification to begin this journey. What you do need is to tap into inner inspiration, passion, and purpose, to believe in yourself, and to enjoy the way. Thoughts will crystalize as you become aware, integrating, transforming your way of life into a new Eco-Conscious Lifestyle. One Room at a Time—one book at a time!

How to Use This Book

Choose where to begin to Release, Renew, Revitalize your bathroom. I suggest starting with the first chapter, which naturally transitions into the following stage. Each chapter brings forth something new.

We will . . . create, be, and do action-inspiring change so you will need a pencil and *The Bathroom* Book.
We will . . . share stories of substance so you will need a pencil and *A Timeless Keepsake*.
I will . . . share with you how . . .

to . . .	*so you can* . . .
embrace your story style	willingly welcome greater **purpose**.
remove toxins	**release** with ease.
begin a new approach	grow to **renew**.
declutter, let go	free yourself to **revitalize**.
organize, arrange, tidy up	enfold in rhythmic **harmony**.
do breathe-able cleaning	celebrate with **joy** the breath of life.
design with purpose	pull your style story together with **passion**.
be conscious of water	preserve our natural resources and with **awareness** raise your vibration.
design a treasure chest of well-being	tap into green beauty with intention to **manifest** your inner light.

ENTER ... 7

Terms to Guide—According to Charisse Marci

Breathe-able	Able to breathe. The ability to breathe clean, therapeutic, transformational air to enhance well-being, your home, and our Earth to truly live a beautiful Eco-Conscious, Healthy-Living Lifestyle.
Eco-consciousness	To be aware of inner thoughts and emotions, for that is what we attract and manifest. To be mindful, respect, and protect all life and our natural and built environment. Synonyms: awareness * mindfulness * ability to recognize * enlightenment . . .

Meet the Icons

Two icons appear throughout the book. The clipboard with pen symbolizes a timeless commitment and bond, and the stacked books with cup is regarded as a symbol of remembrance. Their purpose is to guide you toward using the corresponding interactive sections and journal.

The clipboard with pen eagerly waits for you at various key spots in every chapter. When you see this icon, it is your cue to take action-inspiring steps. Simply follow along.

The stacked books with cup eagerly awaits you at the closing of each chapter. When you see this icon, it is a cue to go to your copy of *A Timeless Keepsake*. Journal bathroom stories from years gone by, tap into the vibe of the present, or imagine what is yet to come.

I suggest sharing this book, *The Bathroom,* with other members of your household. Each household member—whether a child, teenager, or adult—will enjoy their own personal copy of *A Timeless Keepsake*.

When you see this icon, it's your turn to enter personal information in *The Bathroom*

answer questions
create lists
add notes
include photos
add recipes
share

When you see this icon, it's your turn to share a personal story in *A Timeless Keepsake*

Your wishes and desires will transform into an action-inspiring journey as you Release, Renew, Revitalize.

ENTER ··· 9

Meet ChaCha

ChaCha is an extension of Charisse Marei. She manifested through thought, my thought. She is the modern-day representation of a fairy—good-natured, vibrant, and whimsical. Her purpose is to guide you along a personal transformational journey to manifest a fabulous Eco-Conscious, Healthy-Living Lifestyle.

Symbolically, she senses your wish for change and travels effortlessly to your home. She enters in preparation to lift spirits and encourage the change you seek—one step at a time, one room at a time. Your entire being will radiate as you travel the path to Release, Renew, Revitalize.

With this book in hand, you will feel ChaCha's guidance along an awakening path to reflect your new journey. Take delight in her uplifting spirit, for it will inspire lasting change for you, children, furry friends, and our Earth.

ChaCha is your personal guide.
She brings light wherever you reside.

Set an intention.
Believe.
Be action-inspiring.

Behold the transformation as your vision manifests into reality.

ChaCha Bracelet

The ChaCha Bracelet is more than an aesthetically enchanting *au naturel* bracelet. It is a treasure of health-giving attributes and a symbolic representation of your intention. Each precious gem is infused with positive vibration and beautiful earth energy. The joining of the beads is intended to raise your conscious awareness, to enhance well-being, and to soothe your mind.

Gracefully cup the handmade bracelet in both hands.
Visualize your personal intention.
Believe in the manifestation of your intention.
Place the ChaCha bracelet around your wrist.

With purpose, choose a pure essential oil.
Dab on the sea glass pendant supporting the three dangling minis.
Breathe in the aromatic qualities.
Feel your intention begin to blossom.

The trio of dangling ancient Roman glass minis are essential.
They represent the 3Rs.
A vivid reminder to bring forth your intention to
Release, Renew, Revitalize.

*With each velvety touch
and mindful glance
your special intention resurfaces.
It speaks to you.*

ChaCha Bag

The ChaCha Bag is quite special. You see, it was designed with you in mind. It's a treasure of health-giving attributes—handmade with love, purpose, and sustainable materials.

Its purpose on the outside is to be seen in a glimpse.
A visual reminder to keep you intentionally moving forward.
To lift spirits.
To Release, Renew, Revitalize.

Its purpose on the inside is to organize the traveling transformational tools in one place.
It's chic and functional.
It speaks to you.

ChaCha Bag

Contents
The Bathroom
A Timeless Keepsake
tablet * USB diffuser *
* pencil * measure * swatches
color cards * water bottle

Be action-inspiring.
Behold the transformation as your vision manifests into reality.

My Story

I believe in the value of sharing to create meaningful, lasting relationships. For this purpose, each chapter commences with my personal story, shared as I remember it and tied in nicely with the chapter contents. At each chapter's closing, I invite you to share a heartfelt story in your journal, *A Timeless Keepsake*. Enjoy a sampling of what to expect.

My Story

How I View Togetherness

The year was 1968. At the delightful age of six, I was bursting with dreams, curiosity, and an abundance of energy. Shortly after Christmas, taking ownership of my sister Johanne's new 45 rpm record player put an extra skip to my step. A varied genre of pop, jazz, soul, and rock brought music to my soul and energy to my feet. Choreographing skits with my brother Derrick came with ease along with performing for our parents. As a young child, I believed my destiny in life was to be an actress, a performer on stage. Bedtime was my special "me time" to imagine, to dream of the life I wished for.

I placed the mini record player on the floor next to my side of the bed. You see, our home was small. We siblings shared bedrooms, and I shared a double bed with Johanne. There were no headsets available. So the volume was set low for only my soul to feel, to hear the music. I gently placed the arm on the edge of the record; the music began to play. I began to dream. I envisioned myself with other young performers jubilantly flowing to dance moves to our choreographed number, captivating the audience. It was then, in the creation of my dreams, that I understood the importance of each performer's role.

It's the equivalent of each interlocking puzzle piece joining together. Every piece unquestionably essential and of equal value regardless of size, shape, or position. This awakening continues to live within me and to surround my being.

I understand the value of togetherness and the importance of each person's role in life. My series, One Room at a Time, is based on togetherness. Together we will learn, we will grow, making a difference embracing, enhancing all life.

I am filled with inspiration and joy as we begin this new journey together!

I ask: regardless of your gender or age, what does togetherness mean to you?

Preparation to Journal

Before beginning each personal journal entry, remember to . . .

1. gather *A Timeless Keepsake* and pencil.
2. select a pure essential oil to enhance the mood—awaken, calm, inspire.
3. allow the gentle flowing mist from essential oils to permeate the breathe-able air. Choose a special quiet place to get cozy, sit peacefully, and breathe deeply.
4. remove external noise, just for a short time while you write.
5. place several drops of essential oil over your heart chakra.
6. take a few moments to transition into relaxation. Permit breath to be center stage. Close your eyes. Breathe in deeply. Set free wondering thoughts of the day.
7. place an intention.
8. slowly, consciously breathe in deep breaths through your nose, hold, and release, breathing out through your mouth. Repeat three times.

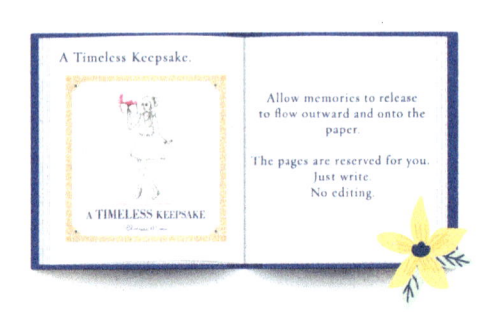

May joy swirl within your being as you awaken hidden treasures from childhood bathroom memories.

14 • • • *Introduction*

We are ready to take the next step together.
On to Chapter 1!

1

The Bathroom

PURPOSE

Remember, then, the four laws of happiness and success.

Count your blessings.
Proclaim your rarity.
Go another mile.
Use wisely your power of choice.
And one more, to fulfill the other four
Do all things with love.

Your are the greatest miracle in the world.

— Og Mandino

My Story

My First Bathroom | 1961–1980

My parents recall the crisp, cool air on a particular October day. The year was 1961. With a skip in their steps and joy in their hearts, they turned the key to open the door of our new home, which they'd purchased six months earlier.

The newly developed Norris Hills Community consisted of hundreds of twin-style homes lining and interlinking the tree-lined streets like soldiers. Our new home sat at the lowest point on the perimeter of the main road leading into the community. The facade faced out and upward to neighboring houses, deciduous trees, and perfectly manicured lawns.

Only segments of the land historically dedicated to farming remained. The earthiness stemming from the soil and the crispness of pure, clean air permeated the senses. Picturesque views from the rear of the house were a welcome sight for the soul. One could hardly miss how the flourishing oak tree, prominently placed on the outer bank, effortlessly snugged the burbling creek. Its long, flowy branches, outstretched at varying degrees, displayed lavish, lush greenery and was home to our feathered friends.

As my parents stood at the threshold, no words were exchanged, though their aura radiated pure bliss. I felt the love, as babies do, in the beat of my mother's heart as she held my tiny six-month-old body close to hers. Today, a new world awaited.

As a family, we represented a traditional, blue-collar, working middle-class, Caucasian, Roman Catholic family. Our unit consisted of one set of parents, John and Elizabeth, my two elder sisters, Celeste and Johanne, my elder brother, John (Eddie), and Derrick, my younger brother.

The architectural design of our twin-style house was based on one prototype. Minor aesthetic exceptions were apparent. A splash of color expressing a homeowner's individuality appeared in exterior details—shutters, doors, and brick facing. Interior design finishes were personalized with lavish embellishments—a splash of color here, a brushstroke there, custom wallpaper, a sprawling sofa, window treatments. Each appointment was truly a reflection of the homeowner's personal style and personality.

The function and dimensions of interior rooms were standard, no additions or changes allowed. Each level had a specific purpose:

Main floor plan	public space; formal living room with side entry and one closet, dining room, kitchen, powder room
Upper floor plan	private space; one narrow hallway, three bedrooms (with one closet each), one bathroom, one linen closet
Lower level floor plan	transitional space; front entrance, attached garage, laundry room, heater room, family room, rear exit

No fluff rooms!

The cycle of remodeling the interior and exterior of our home had a beginning but no end. A new makeover project was initiated One Room at a Time.

Mother was the interior designer, fabricator, and general contractor. Skilled laborers consisted of family, such as aunts and uncles, who joined together on each project with a set of tools, homemade meals, and musical instruments. The various sounds of sewing machines humming, hammers tapping, and people laughing, singing, and chatting remain embedded as a forever memory.

The lower-level redesign expressed a fully functional, open floor plan for personal and creative use. The back section embraced seating for relaxation and entertainment purposes. A workshop took precedence over the remaining frontal space (formerly the garage.) Propped in the center of the floor were my grandfather's two hand-carved wooden horses and refurbished sheets of plywood. Each of the pieces were assembled to create a sixteen-by-eight-foot worktable. This is where ideas blossomed and production took place.

I wonder how Mother did it? With no formal education, she naturally and effortlessly transformed the interior of our house into a home. With few sketches in hand, construction commenced. Walls went up and walls came down. Various wall applications such as paint, wallpaper, and stucco were applied throughout our home. Her motto was Learn as You Go.

Mother's original designs were in abundance, keeping everyone busy. Chalk lines on the table, sewing machines in motion, and the standard needle, thread, and thimble led to the production of window dressings, bedding and bath ensembles, wearable fashions, and accessories. She also designed our kitchen table, master bed, and interior wrought iron gates. One by one, each room transformed from four walls and a floor into house beautiful.

I've since learned that my mother was designing and fabricating fashions at the tender age of eight. Her talents were admired by my great-aunt Betty, a fashion designer and the owner of a department store in New York City. Aunt Betty had the pleasure of designing hats for Lilly Daché while traveling the world in style. Her wish was to bring my mother to NYC to live and to learn the fashion industry. Mother declined the offer.

Just think — if she had gone to New York, neither my siblings nor I would exist.

Expenses generated for renovations were paid in cash from a sole source of income. At the time, our father's weekly net pay was a mere seventy-two dollars. Imagine. Yet there was no debt, no unfulfilled needs. Clearly, I was unaware of our financial limitations. With ease our house transformed into a home with all the necessary amenities.

Health + Wellness = Happiness!

Values

Thirty-seven years have passed since I first left home . . . oh so quickly! I recall the single flight of stairs in the formal living room leading to the upper floor of our home. While climbing the carpet-lined stairs, I could hear the movement of hands on the analog clock. Hanging with authority on the far wall at the top of the stairs was the memorable two-foot-square, battery-operated clock with black and gold trimmings. The clock provided a conditional or unconditional welcome to one's arrival.

The hallway was short and narrow. One area provided space enough for a French provincial buffet table constructed of fruitwood. Mounted above was a gracious rectangular mirror framed in maple wood. I close my eyes now and see myself standing before the buffet table, staring down into our family Bible, whose beautiful, awe-inspiring, lifelike color images never ceased to capture my attention. The bathroom and master bedroom were the anchor to the hallway, with the bathroom at the front of the house and master bedroom at the rear.

For sixteen years, seven people shared the same bathroom every day. Order, timing, neatness, and respect were an absolute must for positive energy and unity to flow smoothly in our home. Each day began with the same orderly routine to use the bathroom. Seniority always ruled. Father, being an early riser and the breadwinner of the family, showered before the sun rose.

Interestingly, I have no recollection of Mother using the bathroom, yet each morning in the kitchen, I admired her beautiful, flawless, and fashionable image. Celeste, the oldest and the commander-in-chief, systematically dictated orders to the younger siblings. Somehow she managed to take the longest time in the bathroom.

Our tiny five-by-seven-foot bathroom was the room in which I learned valuable disciplines, forming lifelong habits and lasting memories. Three of the most memorable memories remain encapsulated in my mind:

- Celeste's daily ritual of announcing, with rhythmic knocking on the door, "Time is up!"
- Derrick and me laughing in the bathtub while forming long extensions—and doggy-ear hairstyles—with soap bubbles;
- My mother, sisters, and me wrapping our hair in bath towels, then draping hand towels over our heads while slowly lowering our faces, one at a time, over the gurgling facial sauna.

During my nineteen years of living in our family home, I have no recollection of remodeling one room in particular: the bathroom. This makes me wonder, was the bathroom considered a room of significance during the 1960s? No one discussed the bathroom. Yet there is so much substance, so much wealth, and countless memories contained in this small, unspoken-of room.

The floor space consisted of a random pattern of tiny one-by-one-inch matte tiles in brown, tan, and cream. Coordinating four-inch glazed brown square tiles uniformly lined the shower walls. To pull it all together, a coat of semi-gloss orange paint was applied to the remaining wall space.

The operable skylight, positioned directly overhead, was my connection to the natural world—heaven, earth, and me. Naturally, when I looked up, I looked beyond to see the light.

Coordinating accessories were meticulously placed with purpose. Seven brown cotton bath towels were folded lengthwise, in thirds, and hung from seven gold rings on the wall directly behind the door. Our names were clearly marked one inch above each ring in gold-and-black lettering. Every third day—no more often, to conserve longevity, natural resources, laundry products, and money—the towels were removed to swish in the washing machine.

With pencil and paper in hand, Mother designed and then fabricated the soft goods to complete the bathroom style story. The cotton shower curtain showcased a whimsical embroidered letter "J" in brown thread. A fluffy beige ensemble (comprised of toilet tank and seat cover with ties) and floor mats softened the feel of the bathroom. A brown wooden desk redesign intentionally transformed into a wall-hanging vanity top with a center drawer. Nestled under the vanity was a small rectangular wicker hamper that served a dual purpose—soiled clothing storage and vanity seat. The seat was topped with a plush cushion and adorned in a comfy fabric for tush delight, and the inside was lined and tied into place with a coordinating removable canvas fabric. A miniature orange Chinese lantern hung over the vanity to complete the composition.

Everyday essentials were carried in daily and placed on the toilet seat, on the vanity top, and in the sink. The products brought into the bathroom to prepare for our day and end our day were also carried out, leaving no trace of daily rituals. No room for clutter.

Bringing your style story together in the bathroom matters. It is a reflection of how you feel as you Release, Renew, Revitalize.

Before You Begin

Childhood memories of the bathroom form a lasting impression in our hearts, our minds, our value systems, and much more. Elevate the grandeur of your recollections as you transfer thoughts into written form in the journal. This is a simple yet rewarding task.

Do you know that each memory recall brings forth an unexpected gift to your soul? As you take the journey to memory, grand emotions will flourish.

You may laugh, you may cry.
You may connect the dots to unfold a fuzzy truth.
You may choose to open the journal to share memories
of the bathroom or hold them secretly close to your heart.

As I began to share stories with my family, we discovered our memories were unique to us, even though we shared one bathroom. How exhilarating to notice the common thread of each person bursting with enthusiasm, eager to chime in with a most favored memory. Who would have imagined sharing memories of the bathroom would bring our family closer together?

Will you choose to share stories of the bathroom? With whom? A parent, sibling, friend, child, or grandchild?

Do note . . .
You hold in your possession a secret key personalized and secured with your inscription. You decide when to open, turn, and design the pages.

inspire

A Standard Design with an Aesthetic Flair

The sketch is a representation from memory of my first bathroom's floor plan.

Floor plan
6'L x 6'W x 8'H

A single door is the transition point leading into the bathroom.

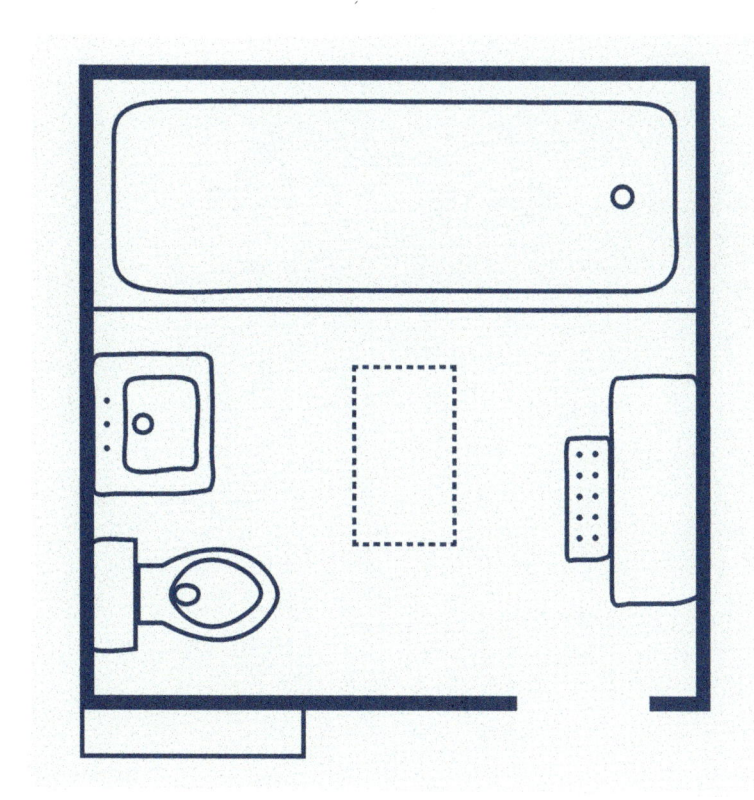

Staple Pieces
simple & minimal

- toilet
- wall-mounted sink
- bathtub/shower combination
- light fixture
- skylight
- recessed medicine cabinet with mirror
- redesign: mini dressing table

Sketch & List

Staple Pieces
simple & minimal

Values Learned

- Proper cleansing etiquette.
- Laughter comes from simplicity.
- How to pamper myself in what I refer to today as "me time."
- How to share a tiny space.
- How to manage time.
- How to respect family members.
- To respect the cleanliness, tidiness, and organization of space.
- Beauty begins from within.

Values learned

Now I Know

- The announcement of the title of this book brought forth curiosity from family and friends.
- Mother never realized the impact her training had on us. She said, "There were no instructions on how to raise children. I went through each day trying to do my best."
- Brother John promptly showered after our father.
- In 1961, Mother and Jeannie (dear friend) "bought that ugly clock at Goldenberg's, a fine furniture store in town."
- Father shared a memory of his first bathroom. "The only means to access a bedroom was through the bathroom. There were no doors and nine siblings. Imagine that!"
- Brother Derrick thought he was a man at the impressionable age of six by taking the razor to his upper lip to shave an invisible hair. A scar remains to this day.
- "**A splash of color**" is my signature phrase.

Now I know

My experience while writing "My Story" provides clarity concerning the person I am today. I absorbed many disciplines during my formative years. I learned basic principles of interior design, yoga, "me time," conservation, etiquette, and respect. I developed a sense of appreciation and connection with our natural and constructed environment. The harmonic vibrational energies set forth allow me to steadily embrace balance and harmony with pure love, utopia. The unifying factor in the forthcoming chapters stems from these basic essential elements learned from childhood.

Your Story

Thoughts to Guide Your Thinking

- Inner inspiration is key to past, present, and future joy . . .
- A room is more than a room . . .
- Memories last a lifetime and beyond . . .

What childhood bathroom memory pops into mind?

We are ready to take the next step together.
On to Chapter 2!

2

Out with the Old

RELEASE

If you could do
just one thing—
make one
conscious choice—
that can change the world,
go organic....
Stop using chemicals.

—Maria Rodale

My Story
The Grocery Store

As a child, I had yet to discover what I came to know as a young adult. You see, my awareness of toxic chemicals began with a memory of the grocery store.

The year was 1967. My personality was a reflection of an enthusiastic, healthy, happy six-year-old with a high metabolism and a tall, skinny frame. An all-too-familiar rhythmic bounce in my walk made way to an exaggerated free-form swing of the poofy ponytail atop my head. These attributes were a mini reflection of my carefree disposition. Life was a depiction of bliss.

As with most stories an exception to the norm prevails. I will explain. You see, the story takes place in the grocery store and what came to be known as "the chemical aisle."

Our mother's role was to guide us five children and manage our home. She orchestrated her motherly role and the seven days of the week with consistency and love in a timely, orderly fashion. Her Friday to-do list included a visit to the salon, a social visit with our grandparents, and grocery shopping. Derrick and I tagged this day as the highlight of the week. I was mostly intrigued with going to the local Genuardi's Family Market. The two locations we frequented reflected unity: small, clean, aromatic, orderly, and friendly.

Each Friday morning the details of the day were set in motion. The day began with personal formalities such as cleanliness, grooming, and selecting spiffy fashions. After breakfast we gathered coupons, paper, and pencil to formulate an itemized grocery list, per item cost, and savings. We eagerly gathered the Green Stamps savings books to proudly carry to the market.

As we entered the store, a dashing gentleman greeted us with a friendly smile and a welcoming hello. We prepared ourselves to embark down each aisle, never missing a one. Mom pushed the shopping cart and Derrick sat in the seat. I stood on the back, ready to hop off, grab the item, and hand it to Derrick, who methodically placed each item in the grocery cart. Our cart was always in order—a habit each of us practices to this day.

While skipping through the first aisle, my senses were aroused by bursts of color and mouth-watering citrus scents that sprang from an array of fresh fruits and vegetables. The aroma of freshly baked bread and cold cuts naturally diffused through the air. Each grouping purposely adorned the display cases, resembling a masterpiece of fine art.

A small piece of paradise indeed!

As we entered the cereal aisle, I excitedly looked for Lucky Charms, Life, and Cream of Wheat. Today, I know better.

We continued up and down each aisle until we entered the one aisle that turned me into a toxic mess! Not again! We rolled our way down the seemingly endless aisle of synthetic bathroom cleaners, floor cleaners, air fresheners, drain cleaners, and laundry soaps. The products towered over my small frame and lined the shelves from top to bottom, front to back, right to left.

My throat tightened. I clasped my throat with both hands to soothe the oncoming feeling. A tickle in the depths of my throat slowly, relentlessly increased. I swallowed hard and wished for it to stop. I cleared my throat, but to no avail; the tickle transformed into a cough. It was bigger than I. Uncontrollable! Tears swiftly streamed down my now-reddened face. I gasped for air as I sat on the floor, feeling hopeless.

What was happening to me? I was fine until I reached the chemical aisle. The all-too-familiar pattern continued for years. Eventually, I hopped off the cart to bypass the chemical aisle.

I referred to the cleaning products aisle as the chemical aisle back then, and today the name remains the same. As a young mother in my twenties, I ran down the chemical aisle with my shopping cart and three children, quickly grabbing items while holding my breath.

On a subliminal level I knew back then, as I consciously know today, that indoor toxic pollutants are harmful to me, my family, our furry friends, our home, and our Earth. My body responded as though I were sick; my smile and laughter momentarily disappeared.

I no longer use any of them, not one. When the tickle starts, I know there is danger around. I hold my breath and run!

Through education, research, and hands-on application,
I discovered a greener, healthier, happier lifestyle.

Before You Begin

I purposefully chose the placement of this chapter toward the beginning of the book, for it is imperative to purge the toxic "stuff," before bringing in eco-friendly products.

I am inclined to share a behind-the-scenes secret with you. The original contents of this chapter were painstakingly written to include toxic product names and full descriptions. I then created colorful designs to place near each description. After a restless night of flipping like a fish out of water, I awakened with clarity and tossed it into the wastebasket. The words written were in opposition to the desired image for this book, which is high-spirited zest. Instead, I chose to use not one toxic word to guide you through this journey of enlightenment to be rid of harmful toxic substances.

Along your journey, always be mindful of the 3Rs, for I coined the unity of these uplifting words with purpose. You see, they replace negative words such as "stress." Apply them to all areas of life as you wish.

Release ... to set free
Renew ... to give fresh life
Revitalize ... to inspire new life

You are ready to empower yourself with uplifting knowledge to get rid of toxic substances. Enjoy the process as you transform—the space you live in, your being, our Earth.

K.I.S.S. = Keep It Simple, Sweetie!
IAQ = Indoor Air Quality

Your Home

Have you given thought to the alarming number of harmful, chemical-laden cleaning products in your linen closet, under the bathroom sink, and perhaps in the shower? It's distressing to realize each spritz and squeeze of a bottle contributes to poor indoor air quality (IAQ). It doesn't stop there. As you breathe in a plethora of fine mist particulates, it affects your inner health and triggers a host of sensitivities.

A mini home quiz

- How many toxic cleaners does it take for your bathroom to sparkle and shine?
- Are you inhaling the all-too-familiar bleach scent with synthetic citrusy fragrances?
- Are you inhaling liquid substances to clear drains?
- Are you using an ammonia-based glass cleaner?
- Have you read the ingredients on all the products you use?
- Can you pronounce the words?
- Do you have a dictionary on hand?
- Have you read the precautionary warning labels?
- Do you skim over the hazard symbols?
- Are you prepared for an emergency situation from chemical-laden mishaps?
- Will you think clearly while in crisis mode?

I encourage you to stand.
Walk, skip, hop, or run to the cleaning closet.
Open a bottle of your most-often-reached-for, chemically formulated household cleaner.
Breathe in deeply (at your own risk).

I ask . . . is this you?

- Gasping for air?
- Light-headed?

- ❏ Dizzy?
- ❏ Coughing?
- ❏ Irritated eyes?
- ❏ All of the above!

Next, walk, skip, hop, or run to the kitchen.
Reach for a fresh lemon, preferably organic.
Slice the lemon in half.
Are your taste buds doing a dance?
Breathe in deeply.

or . . . is this you?

- ❏ An aha moment!
- ❏ Taste bud stimulating!
- ❏ A smile!
- ❏ Able to breathe in again!
- ❏ _____!
- ❏ All of the above!

This simple mini home quiz brings sensory awareness to the forefront of your mind.
The choice is yours.

Your Body

How many chemical-laden personal care products does it require for you to look, feel, and smell synthetically uplifted, in order to "take on your day," as talk show host Dr. Laura says? Personal care products include everything from facial and hair care, to lotions, to perfumes and cologne, to personal hygiene. Let's not forget cosmetics.

Your skin, the largest organ of your body, absorbs applied substances. These substances enter your bloodstream, and, in turn, your internal organs. Wow! What if you could tally all those chemicals in weight per month, per year? You may want to reread before layering another dose of synthetic cream all over your body and those of your children.

Let's do a memory recall. Imagine yourself taking a shower with the water turned a bit to the hotter side to create a warm, steamy, isolated space. You climb in, dismissing the unlovable water smell. You lather up your hair with a chemical-laden, scented shampoo. You lather up your body with a similar body wash. It smells so delightful that you cup your sudsy hands under your nose and breathe in deeply. Ahh!

In the meantime, your lungs and pores are wide open, absorbing the toxins like a sponge. You begin to feel a bit light-headed and slightly dizzy. Is this from hunger, the steamy hot shower, chlorinated water, personal care products, or all of the above?

· ·

A mini body quiz

❑ Have you read the ingredients in your personal care products?
❑ Do the ingredients contain harmful synthetic chemicals?

How many chemical-laden personal care products are in the . . .
❑ bathtub
❑ beauty containers
❑ closets
❑ drawers
❑ shelves
❑ shower

❑ toilet room
❑ vanity

❑ Did you choose them for the delightful smell?
❑ Were you captivated by the attractive advertisement?
❑ How many synthetic substances does your skin absorb daily?

❑ Have you thought about why you simply do not feel good?
❑ Do you recall feeling light-headed while taking a warm/hot shower?

Do you think this is from . . .
❑ a steamy hot shower?
❑ chemical-laden bathing products?
❑ chlorinated water?
❑ hunger?

I encourage you to stand.
Walk, skip, hop, or run to the bathroom.
Reach for your shampoo, hair spray, perfume, or cologne bottle.
Take the top off.
Breathe in deeply (at your own risk).

I ask . . . is this your immediate response?

❑ Gasping for air?
❑ Light-headed?
❑ Dizzy?
❑ Coughing?
❑ Irritated eyes?
❑ All of the above!

Did you experience a delayed response?
- ❑ Headache?
- ❑ Vertigo?
- ❑ Irritating rash?
- ❑ An hour from now?
- ❑ Hours from now?
- ❑ All of the above!

*The time is now to let go . . .
of harmful cleaning & personal care products!*

Bye-Bye Toxic Chemicals

At rest we breathe about
16 breaths per minute
960 breaths per hour
23,040 breaths per day
8,409,600 breaths per year.

If we live to eighty,
we breathe about
672,768,000 breaths.

This is good! As long as the breathe-able air is nourishing your being, home, furry friends, and our Earth. So I ask you, how clean is the air you breathe in your home? How clean is the air going into your lungs? Are you breathing in toxic pollutants or deliciously healthy, aromatic air?

You read about it, you hear about it: our indoor air can be up to five times more polluted than the air we breathe outside. We spend, on average, 80 percent of our time indoors breathing harmful, unhealthy pollutants. As of this writing, full ingredient disclosure is not required on countless household and personal care products. That is pretty scary since the home is considered a safe haven to live, love, and renew with zest!

The fantastical news: you opened the door to mindfully journey into an Eco-Conscious, Healthy-Living Lifestyle to Release, Renew, Revitalize with purpose.

Put on comfy walking shoes, for we are about to venture through your home and garage to take inventory of toxic cleaners. I recommend taking before, in progress, and after pictures. Why? It is easy to forget the initial inventory of chemical-laden products existing in your home. Photos are a way to see the entire transformation from the initial toxic inventory to the final makeover touch.

Let's begin with chemical-laden cleaners for the bathroom, followed by personal care products. Open every closet, cabinet, drawer, container, and shelf where you store these products and supplies. Make certain to include products promoting "eco-friendly," "natural," "green," and "nontoxic."

Gather them to one central area. Place products on a large surface—the kitchen table or a countertop.

The Labels

To learn about labels is empowering. With your newfound awareness, the ability to identify harmful, chemical-laden products will be a breeze. The expression "If all else fails, read the labels, read the instructions" holds true. Reading labels provides a plethora of information even when the list of ingredients appears to have little to no meaning to you.

The phrase "A picture is worth a thousand words" is all telling. I thought it best to visit the local grocery store for a hands-on experience to read the labels and look for signal words and phrases on toxic containers. (Typically, I avoid this aisle, as you have already discovered.) From the beginning to the end of the aisle, there was no shortage of products with labels bearing signal words and phrases; they were everywhere.

Lining the shelves from the very top to the very bottom were countless brands of superlative cleaning products. Colorfully labeled products, strategically marketed, claiming they can transform your stinky, dirty home into a sparkly clean, perfume-scented haven. All were within reach.

In your mind you can hear them scream, "Pick me!"

Now imagine yourself in the grocery store in this very aisle. You spot the new air freshener. With a skip in your step, your heels lift off the floor as you reach on the tippy-top shelf for the attractive yet, simply designed air freshener scented with a yummy citrus blend. Your memory bank replays the recently viewed commercial of the jubilant woman breathing in the fresh fragrance as she generously sprays the contents in dance-like form. As whimsical thoughts of delightful freshness swirl about in your mind, you joyfully place the container in the basket and continue on, mindlessly.

Did you read the label?

Did you see the uppercase, bold text? DANGER, WARNING, CAUTION, KEEP OUT OF REACH OF CHILDREN. FLAMMABLE, EYE IRRITANT.

Did you read the ingredients?

Or does this sound familiar? I glance at the unrecognizable list of ingredients, roll over the unpronounceable words. To understand them, I need a magnifying glass and a dictionary. A basic training class is needed in this aisle as well. The "whatever" attitude sets in as you reach for yet another familiar yet toxic cleaning product.

Here we are, in the present, staring at your collection of chemical-laden cleaners. Observe closely what warnings are on those containers. How many bottle labels bear a signal word, such as "caution," "warning," "danger," "extreme danger," "corrosive," "poison," or "irritant"? Do you see hazard symbols or phrases, for instance "Keep out of reach of children," and "Vapors harmful?"

Even labels promoting "green," "eco-friendly," "environmentally friendly," "natural" and "non-toxic" may have toxic synthetic ingredients lurking inside. Please note: as of the writing of this book, the healthier terms are not yet regulated by the FDA.

The labels neatly package information—directions, ingredients, storage, safety, and proper disposal. Labels warn of immediate effects from breathing in fumes, swallowing, direct contact with skin, eye exposure, and so on.

I ask . . .
- How do you keep little fingers out of the mouth?
- How do you stop furry friends from licking those paws?
- How many chemicals are you exposed to daily?
- Is the harm from exposure long-lasting or could it be fatal?
- What about factors such as your health and age?

Personal care products and cosmetic labels also bear warning and caution statements. Do note: the list of ingredients is in descending order of concentration. The truth is, the brands you love and trust may contain harmful ingredients that adversely affect well-being, your home, and our Earth.

The key is to know what to look for and to . . .

K.I.S.S.
Keep It Simple, Sweetie!

Identify key signal words, phrases, or symbols that are predominant on the front label of each product. Additional cautions are on the bottom, reverse side, and/or inside packaging. Read the precautionary labels in their entirety. In the process you will learn how to safely store and dispose of chemical-laden products.

ChaCha gasps!
She quickly flees past products with caution words and phrases!

The Signal Words

Be aware of products bearing signal words. The level of toxicity in each product is determined by the "signal word."

CAUTION!	Slightly toxic	An ounce to a pint
WARNING!	Moderately toxic	A teaspoon to an ounce
DANGER!	Highly toxic	A taste to a teaspoon

I recall my first-year architectural professor explaining how to see a building: "You see, and then you see." Clearly, it is how you look at the subject matter. One may see a building while another sees the fine details. Since then, I apply this motto to every aspect of life. Ask yourself, "How many times have I strolled the household chemical aisle, picked up a can or spray bottle of cleaner, and placed it into my cart, never noticing the bold, uppercase signal words and phrases?"

RELEASE ··· 45

Now you know. Now you will see. You've got the picture! Regardless of the level of toxicity, these products are toxic and cause harm! Eliminate the precautions by eliminating all toxic products from your home and outside environment.

With a new awareness of reading labels, you will consciously take notice of various hazard symbols. The hazard symbols are precautions to prevent dangerous health concerns topically, internally, and within the home.

In four simple steps, you will learn how to identify specific symbols, types of hazards, and associated meanings. Share this newfound awareness with everyone in your household!

Hazard Symbols for Household Cleaning Products

1. Look for **the symbol** to know the meaning.

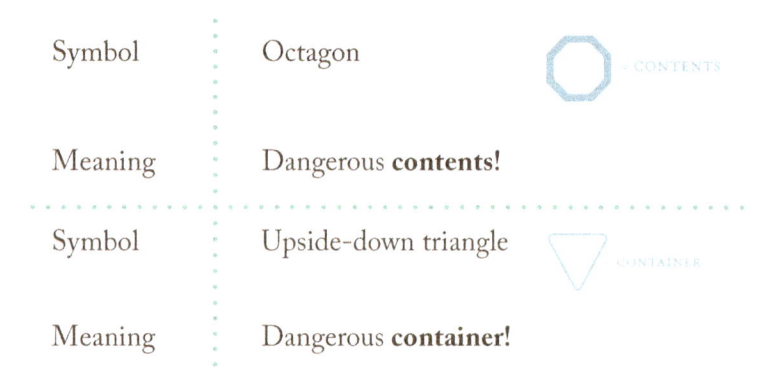

Symbol	Octagon
Meaning	Dangerous **contents**!
Symbol	Upside-down triangle
Meaning	Dangerous **container**!

2. Look **inside the symbol** for the type of hazard—octagon or upside-down triangle.

Out with the Old

3. Be conscious of the **types of hazards** and the meaning behind the symbol.

Symbol		Corrosive
Meaning		Danger! May cause seriously dangerous conditions topically and internally at point of contact. May also cause damage to materials.
Key phrase		Causes chemical burns. Injurious to skin and eyes.
Bathroom corrosive products		Household cleaners, drain cleaners, toilet bowl cleaners, bleach, laundry stain removers, and so on.
Precaution		Read the label. Handle with caution. Wear protection: gloves, goggles, face mask. May burn, topically and/or internally, skin, eyes, respiratory tract, stomach.
Symbol		Flame
Meaning		Danger! The product/vapor can be flammable even at low temperature.
Key phrase		Keep from heat or flame—extremely flammable, vapor harmful.
Bathroom flammable products		Hair spray, nail polish remover, furniture polish, aerosol paint containers, etc.
Precaution		Read the label. Keep away from heat, sparks, and flames. Wear protection: gloves, goggles, face mask. Wash hands after use.

Symbol		Poison/Toxic
Meaning		Danger! Inhalation, licking, eating, swallowing, and skin absorption can cause serious illness or death.
Key phrase		Harmful or fatal if swallowed. Keep out of reach of children.
Bathroom poisonous products		Furniture polish, pharmaceuticals, bleach, pesticides, cleaning fluids, drain openers, etc.
Precaution		Read the label. Handle with caution. Do not take internally. Do not breathe in vapors. Wear protection: gloves, goggles, face mask. Wash hands after use.
Symbol		Explosive
Meaning		Explosive danger!
Key phrase		Avoid ignition sources.
Bathroom explosive products		Aerosol container paint, aerosol container water repellant for shoes.
Precaution		Do not puncture can. Do not heat can. In doing so, the container can explode, causing injuries. Wear protective clothing.

Out with the Old

4. Look for and identify the symbol located above the **signal word**.

   SIGNAL WORDS | CORROSIVE | FLAMMABLE | POISON | TOXIC | EXPLOSIVE

   Additional Symbols

   Health hazard. Hazardous to the **ozone** layer.

   Serious **health** hazard.

   Hazard to the **environment** and toxic to aquatic organisms.

   Keep out of reach of **children.**

   Beyond the label is the most empowering!

Beyond The Label

Material safety data sheets (MSDS) and the Environmental Working Group website (EWG.org) are two of my favored online resource tools listing full product disclosure.

Both resources are power tools in your toolbox. Research household cleaners, personal care products, and cosmetics to unveil the rating of your beloved products. Then decide which item to eliminate from the household and purchase list forevermore. Share gathered information with family and friends.

MSDS

Four steps to a successful online search.
1. Choose a product.
2. Begin an online search. Enter MSDS and product name. Choose a result.
3. *MSDS categories* lists specific details about the product.
4. Decide if the product stays or goes.

EWG—Household Cleaners

Four steps to a successful online search.
1. Choose a product.
2. Begin an online search. Enter ewg.org/cleaners. Enter product name.
3. *EWG categories* lists specific details about the product. The rating category indicates the level of toxic concern from exposure to the ingredients. An A rating is the least concern and F is the highest.
4. Decide if the product stays or goes.

EWG—Personal Care Products

Four steps to a successful search.
1. Choose a product.
2. Begin an online search. Enter ewg.org/skindeep. Enter product name.
3. *EWG categories* lists specific details about the product.
4. Decide if the product stays or goes.

Notice the score category. Click on the green score symbol to reveal a pop-up window. The EWG-verified mark assures the product meets the EWGs strict health criteria.

The hazard score key advises the level of hazard—lowest (green 1–2), moderate (gold 3–6), and high (red 7–10)—and the green data score key rates the information known about each ingredient—none, limited, fair, good, excellent.

Bring it all together. Return to the chemical-laden products laid out before you. Identify and remove those unhealthy products in four easy steps.

1. Group like with like. Suggestions:

Your home	air fresheners all-purpose cleaners	bleach drain cleaner/openers	soap scum removers toilet bowl cleaners
Your body	aerosols bathing care	cosmetics oral care	perfume/cologne toiletries

2. List all chemical-laden products by name and quantity.
3. Identify signal words, phrases, and symbols on the label.
4. Rate each product.

Turn tasks into an inspiring mission!

Chemical-Laden Products

Be Eco-Conscious, be purposeful, be empowered. Note factual information about "your home" and "your body" products. Make the choice to rid of those toxic products once and for all.

Product	Qty	Signal Words + Phrases	Symbol (draw)	Rate	Cost

Out with the Old

Nasty
hazardous
toxic
ingredients
in bathroom cleaners
home products
personal care products
to avoid?
All of them!

My pledge: to avoid chemical-laden bathroom cleaners, personal care products, and home products.

Pledge please

Storage Safety Etiquette

If you are inclined to keep those unhealthy products, know how to store them. Storing chemical-laden products properly is key to avoid unnecessary, unforeseeable mishaps. Protecting children, furry friends, your home, and our Earth is essential.

consciously thoughtful

- Designate one storage area for all products.
- Store in the garage, basement, or separate storage area.
- Store in original container, secure lids, label, and date.
- Store away from flammable products.
- Store like products with like.
- Separate hazardous materials by type.
- Store on top shelves and inside cabinets. Lock doors.
- Best of all . . . avoid toxic products altogether!

Protection Etiquette

Be proactive! Wear protective clothing and accessories when using household products with signal words, cautionary labels, and symbols. Always protect yourself and those you love. Gather and use the following:

consciously thoughtful

- apron
- footware
- gloves
- mask
- respiratory protection
- safety goggles/safety glasses
- ventilate: open two opposite windows for a cross breeze or use a fan.
- Best of all . . . avoid toxic products altogether!

Out with the Old

Disposal Etiquette

Disposing of toxic chemicals requires strategic thinking. Gone are the days of flushing and pouring chemicals down household drains, in the street, in sewers, and on earthy grass. How scary is the thought of partially full or empty chemical containers landing in the bottom of your wastebasket? When not disposed of properly, the chemical's life is not over. It moves from inside the house to out doors. Disregarding "Disposal Etiquette" hampers all life in our natural and built environment.

consciously thoughtful

- Return unopened products.
- Separate garbage by category—glass, plastic, paper, toxic chemicals.
- Read the label. Follow instructions and guidelines.
- Recycle recyclable containers.
- When in doubt, call the manufacturer.
- Contact your local community for hazardous household product pickup schedules.
- Share how-to with neighbors.
- Best of all . . . avoid toxic products altogether!

Values Learned
- Labels have value.
- Going beyond your comfort zone is gratifying.
- Bye-bye street shoes. Hello, house shoes, socks, and slippers.
- K.I.S.S. This little phrase was introduced to me in 1979 by Mary Ann Fabrizio. Thirty-ish years later, I consciously apply it to daily life.
- Sage and Citrus, my puppies who are otherwise known as "The Girls," love me. My grandbabies love me. They come to my home and it feels good.
- I feel good! You should too!

Values learned

Now I Know

- Less is more.
- Always find the answer to the "why."
- Warning signals: chemical odor, fuzzy head, dizziness, throat tickle, teary eyes.
- Not all cleaning products are created equal.
- No pesticides for the home, inside or out.
- Remove shoes to reduce the amount of chemicals brought into the home.
- Never mask unpleasant odors. Identify, release, replace.
- Avoid products with offensive odors. Take your nose right to it. If it smells like a chemical, do not purchase. Do not bring it into the home.
- Share empowering knowledge with your cleaning service company.

Now I know

Know . . .
Your family and furry friends will love you.
The environment will love you.
Your purse will love you.
You will love you.
That's a lot of love!

Enjoy recommendations and recipes in forthcoming chapters.
K.I.S.S.
DIY
Ready-Made

Your Story

Thoughts to Guide Your Thinking

- Just because you can't see it doesn't mean it's not there . . .
- Breathe-ably delicious air brings a bright, clear sparkle to your eyes . . .
- I see. I feel. I breathe . . .

My most unfavorable memory of chemical exposure is, what?

We are ready to take the next step together.
On to Chapter 3!

3

In with the New

RENEW.....

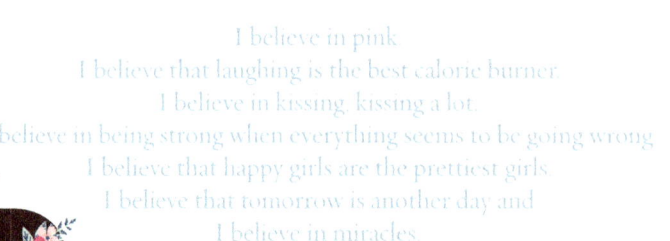

I believe in pink.
I believe that laughing is the best calorie burner.
I believe in kissing, kissing a lot.
I believe in being strong when everything seems to be going wrong.
I believe that happy girls are the prettiest girls.
I believe that tomorrow is another day and
I believe in miracles.

Audrey Hepburn

My Story
A New Me

I've been blessed, since childhood, with inner inspiration and self-motivation. Creating to-do lists came with ease. They were intertwined with everyday life, as were my "Dear God" letters and family interior design projects.

When a new project commenced, we gathered our tools and materials. Our focus never strayed as we worked on tasks at hand until the final details were completed. My parents saw the vision from concept to completion. A plan was in place with an understanding of the minute details. I learned their style and the importance of details early on.

The desire to develop my personal style stirred from within. Transitioning from my parents' technique to developing a new personalized approach was empowering. During the process, I discovered self-renewal and the ability to recognize my accomplishments.

My new approach was interwoven with appreciation. Gratitude was at the forefront of each new day as I strove to increase awareness through my senses. As the sun rises on each new day, my overall approach remained constant with minor tweaking:

I see . . .	myself in the mirror.
I say . . .	good morning, sunshine. You are special. I am grateful for another day to live, laugh, love with zest. To breathe with ease; to feel the warmth of the sun; to love and to be loved; to be passionate, patient, persistent; to learn, to grow, and to guide.

I feel …	confirmation and inner joy as thoughts flourish through my being. Surfacing, radiating until my aura beams with beautiful color extending far beyond my physical stature. Telepathically I feel the urge to send wishes of pure love and protection to my family, especially my grandbabies and "The Girls." I feel positive energy saturate the room and the gaze of Sage through me.
I smell …	the crispness of the morning dew as it blends with the aromatic delights nourishing my being and the breathe-able air.
I hear …	a voice from within that says, "Today, as the day before is a gift. Continue along this path of enrichment, fulfilling your journey to a beautiful Eco-Conscious, Healthy-Living Lifestyle."

I am grateful!

Before You Begin

A new approach = A new you!

From here forward, you are both the interior decorator and the client of your project. Embrace newfound knowledge to empower yourself with basic skills and welcome each project with confidence from the initial planning to completion, but only One Room at a Time! You will receive the necessary Tools of the Trade, as I refer to them, at the appropriate time.

As you transition from chapter to chapter, you will see and you will feel, from the inside out and the outside in, the rewards of the plan you set in motion. By engaging in simple yet effective steps, you are certain to enjoy every stage of the process.

We begin with a pre-consultation—three initial steps that take minutes to do—followed by the initial consultation.

This is your commitment to honor you.

grow

PP = (Charisse's) personal preference

o&t = organization & tidiness

Pre-Consultation

Preparation for the initial consultation is key. This is where the momentum builds. Knowing you are about to embark on an interior design project toward an Eco-Conscious Lifestyle is inspiring. We will identify the areas of interest and level of commitment to establish clarity, focus, balance, and harmony. Let's begin with three doable steps.

1. Identify Your Project

What you choose is what you will do. Is it to declutter, clean, organize, or something else? As you review the list, checkmark each category of interest. The categories will become your projects. With guidance, you will easily transition from one project to the next.

Choose one or choose all!
What you choose is what you will do!

Identify to

- **DECLUTTER** — Remove unnecessary items to free the space and being from clutter and stuff.
- **ORGANIZE** — Arrange into a structured whole. Tidy up!
- **CLEAN** — Free from pollutants and unpleasant substances.
- **REDESIGN** — Take away, add new, and bring it all together with simplicity for a fresh new eco-friendly look.
- **DESIGN** — Draw a basic floor plan. Add essentials for functionality and aesthetics.
- **CONSERVE** — Know the secret to saving money and resources like water and indoor air quality.
- **ME TIME** — Release, Renew, Revitalize!
- **PREPARE** — Don't be caught wishing. Have products stocked and ready!

2. Schedule a Date

This step eliminates procrastination. But more importantly, this step initiates the transformation of your thoughts to paper and to reality. Take a moment to ponder the appointments currently scheduled for the month. The pop-up (thought) bubbles coming to mind may include wellness activities, social events, clients, playdates, and seminars. Take this time to schedule a date with *you* for the bathroom. It's effortless!

Allow one hour for the initial consultation. Do not schedule anything else in this time slot! Do not erase, delete, or change! You have value.

Do it now!

.... is the best day of the week for me.

.... is the best time of the day for me.

.... I am committed to this date.

.... is my committed available time.

3. The Reminder

No excuses. Regardless of your status in life, responsibilities are plentiful as are the endless to-do lists filled with varying tasks of importance. Setting reminders frees the mind to focus on the present. Add a special ring to reminders.

Free your mind.

	Twenty-four hours in advance.
	One hour beforehand.
	I am committed to this date.

You are prepared for the initial consultation.

The Initial Consultation

The initial consultation is in preparation to grasp your project as a whole, to ultimately manifest personal desires and goals. It is presented in three interactive sections:

Section A	Identify Your Approach
Section B	Tools of the Trade
Section C	Set the Stage (inspiring-action)

Reap the rewards of progress each day as you discover certain remarkable facts about yourself and family members. Keep in mind that emotional and physical comfort is essential for moving forward with ease.

To uplift spirits, dab a few drops of an essential oil over your heart chakra and breathe. This sets the tone to reflect beautiful energy from within and in the physical space. It doesn't stop there. Your fabulous energy is felt by others, including your furry friends.

Identify Your Approach

Section A

Identify your approach toward a new project. Are you self-motivated, uncertain, or semi-motivated? Once identified continue with Section A or scooch over to Section B. Either way, move forward with positive energy and confidence.

Tweak accordingly!

Name: Age: Date:

- ❏ Self-Motivated
- ❏ Uncertain
- ❏ Semi-Motivated

❏ Inspiration begins from within.

❏ I welcome change with enthusiasm.

❏ I set obtainable goals.

❏ I begin with a plan.

❏ I start with one section at a time.

❏ Completion excites me.

❏ I am motivated.

❏ I hesitate to start.

❏ How do I begin?

❏ Where do I begin?

❏ So many decisions to make.

❏ I have _____ scheduled for today, but I find myself doing _____ instead.

❏ I will find time tomorrow, next week, next month.

❏ Can't wait to begin.

Scooch right on over to Section B.

Let's identify those unhealthy obstacles preventing you from taking action.

Continue with Section A.

Let's identify those unhealthy obstacles preventing you from taking action.

Continue with Section A.

70 · · · *In with the New*

Identify **Acknowledge** **Release**

- Did you check the uncertain or semi-motivated category?
- Do unhealthy obstacles stump you?
- The time is now to rid yourself of unhealthy obstacles!

Identify	Be true to yourself. Search within (meditate) to identify obstacles preventing you from moving forward. Make reference in your journal with bullet points or complete sentences.
Acknowledge	Yes, these are the reasons preventing me from moving forward with an action-inspiring plan.
Release	Design a ritual to remove negative thought patterns. Put into motion. This is an ideal time to inhale a releasing essential oil. You must believe. In the following chapter I share a personal ritual on how to release internal clutter.

Things to Think About

I begin by believing in my higher self.	I respect my time.
I begin with one chapter at a time.	I have order.
I begin with one section at a time.	I honor myself.
I complete each task.	I honor my word.

Note unhealthy obstacles. Feel free to expand on this subject matter in your journal, A Timeless Keepsake.

What is your intention for addressing change in the bathroom? Write in a short sentence or two.

Your New Journey

Commit	to your new approach. Honor you. Out with the old thoughts and in with the new.
Seek	assistance from a trusted source to help honor your commitment and guide you forward.

Be	a leader. Use *The Bathroom* book for guidance. Join my team and then form a private support group to encourage and implement change. Set a plan in motion.
Diffuse	a therapeutic essential oil to enhance happiness, focus, confidence, inspiration, abundance, and so much more.
Enjoy	the journey one task at a time.

You are well on your way!
Let's move on to Section B!

Section B

Tools of the Trade

Each project requires specific tools to satisfy the task at hand. Essentials range from conventional tools—measure tape, drawing material, and samples to unconventional items—questionnaire and mood enhancers. You will be guided at the appropriate time of what tools to gather. Choose what is needed. No more. No less.

The Toolbox Carrier

A standard toolbox is a sturdy carrying box, container, or chest to store hand tools. Choose one or multiple toolboxes to organize and store essentials.

Over the years I acquired multiple toolboxes of varying designs. My original toolbox is a purple tackle box with sectional interior compartments filled with gadgets from interior design school, hand-me-downs, household projects, and design installations.

As a student of the first Young Living Beauty School, I received a complimentary gift: a transportable, expandable cushioned toolbox complete with green beauty essentials.

Both toolbox designs are purposeful and readily complement organization and tidiness (o&t). Begin with minimal items. Add along the way.

PP: Aluminum train case/expandable/compartments

*The Toolbox carrier is
an expression of your fashion style
and quality of organization!*

What's your toolbox style?

ChaCha Bag

The ChaCha bag is for children, teens, and the young at heart (that's you). Personalize it with specific tools to compliment your individual style. Fill one bag with traveling transformational items. Specify a second bag for soft cleaning essentials—cloths, pouches, apron, and bottle of water.

PP: ChaCha bag

Gaze into the bag.
A past memory will surface.
A new memory is about to take place.

What's in your bag?

Attitude

With each new project, be certain your attitude reflects joy, inspiration, and momentum, reaching the pinnacle upon completion. Recognize, appreciate, and feel the energy of the room. It is a reflection of you.

PP: *Sassy*

Elevate your energy level.
Approach change with enthusiasm.
Positive energy is contagious!

What's your attitude?

Attire

Select comfy clothing for ease of movement and to conform to the task at hand. Avoid nasty push-ins from buttons and zippers while bending, sitting, and stooping. Purchase new or grab favorites from a drawer.

Hair accessories are fashionable and functional. A well-needed specialty item to control hair and prevent facial drips. Slip a headband, wrap a skinny scarf, or wear a jeweled band.

Choose color wisely. Color is all-inspiring and lifts your mood. It's part of your personal style story. My signature style includes a **splash of color!**

PP: T-shirt, leggings, hair band, bare feet, apron

Today's fashion is all about comfort.
Add a "splash of color."
Have fun!

What's your fashion style?

Setting The Mood

Scent

Au naturel, pure, plant-based essential oils are my go-to. I dab a drop behind each ear lobe, over my heart, on my wrists, and through my hair. Since each oil has a purpose, I ask myself, what do I need? What do my furry, fluffy friends need today? I may opt for an oil to enhance clarity, bring joy, or inspire action.

PP: A blend of—lime, cedarwood, vanilla, ocotea, lavender

Breathe in the health attributes of awe inspiring pure, fresh aromatics. Add a "splash of essential oil."

What's your go-to scent?

In with the New

Music

Select a motivational genre to set the mood envisioned. Embrace the rhythm of each instrumental piece. Feel the uplifting mojo as it swirls within and around your sanctuary. Dance a little, move a little, sing out loud. Never stop.

PP: Pop

Embrace the energy of your aura, the room!

What's your genre?

Well done!
Let's move on to Section C!

Initial Consultation Questionnaire

Section C

The questionnaire is designed to understand the present space and to set the stage to embrace change.

My bathroom

- People sharing the bathroom with you.

- Name this bathroom.

- Pets sharing the bathroom with you.

- Do you share the bathroom at the same time?

- What time of the day is mostly spent in this room?

- Can you move around the room with ease?

- Do you need additional space within the space?

- Do you have a floor plan of the bathroom?

- Is the room utilized for a purpose beyond hygiene?

- Additional purpose?

How do you feel in your bathroom?
- ❏ clutter feeling
- ❏ unorganized
- ❏ lack of energy
- ❏ unhappy
- ❏ headachy, stuffy
- ❏ unmotivated
- ❏ light/airy
- ❏ organized
- ❏ energetic
- ❏ happy
- ❏ healthy
- ❏ motivated

How do you feel when a guest requests to use the bathroom?
- ❏ embarrassed
- ❏ hesitant
- ❏ confident

- ❏ Are you ready for eco-friendly, feel-good alternatives?
- ❏ Do you designate a place for products?

Do you . . .
- ☐ routinely search for that one thing?
- ☐ forget what you are looking for?
- ☐ know how to organize?

Are accessories…
- ☐ messy?
- ☐ organized?
- ☐ compartmentalized?
- ☐ clean?
- ☐ like with like?

Are drawers, cabinets, and linen closets . . .
- ☐ messy?
- ☐ organized?
- ☐ compartmentalized?
- ☐ clean?
- ☐ like with like?

- ☐ Is additional storage space a necessity?
- ☐ Are you ready to clear the clutter, organize, and tidy with purpose?

What odors are prominent when entering the room?
- ☐ cleaners
- ☐ cologne/perfume
- ☐ mold
- ☐ poo
- ☐ stinky clothes
- ☐ synthetic air fresheners
- ☐ synthetic candles
- ☐ pure essential oils

Are the staple pieces clean?
- ❏ bathtub
- ❏ sink
- ❏ shower
- ❏ toilet
- ❏ inside
- ❏ outside

Do you have a wastebasket? If so, is it . . .
- ❏ filled?
- ❏ overflowing?
- ❏ odor-filled?
- ❏ aromatic?
- ❏ clean?

- ❏ Are you ready for an eco-friendly solution?
- ❏ Are you ready to switch out chemical-laden products for eco-alternatives?
- ❏ Are you ready to do daily, monthly, and semi-annually spot cleaning and thorough cleaning the eco-friendly way?
- ❏ Do you follow recent trends to design?
- ❏ Are you ready to design your private and semi-private sanctuary with passion?

What changes are needed?

_____

_____

_____

_____

Rewrite in a short sentence or two.

What is your intention with the proposed changes?

Will you hire a contractor or DIY?

What is your timeline?

Success in honoring yourself!

Why I Love My Bathroom

I Feel Good	**I Feel Wishy-Washy**
♦ Identify "Why I love my bathroom."	♦ Identify "Why I am *not* loving my bathroom."
♦ List the five reasons in order of importance to you.	♦ List the five reasons in order of importance to you.
♦ Acknowledgment is good.	♦ Acknowledgment helps you move forward with ease.
♦ Get ready for the next step, an easy climb.	♦ Get ready for the next step.

Why I LOVE My Bathroom

1. _____
2. _____
3. _____
4. _____
5. _____

Acknowledgment

_____
_____

Why I Am *NOT* Loving My Bathroom

1. _____
2. _____
3. _____
4. _____
5. _____

Acknowledgment

_____
_____

I am ready!

Values Learned

- My attitude toward a project is a reflection of my inner self.
- To believe all things happen with and for a purpose is empowering.
- When I clarify my personal style, confidence flourishes with ease.
- I complete each task to honor myself, my word.

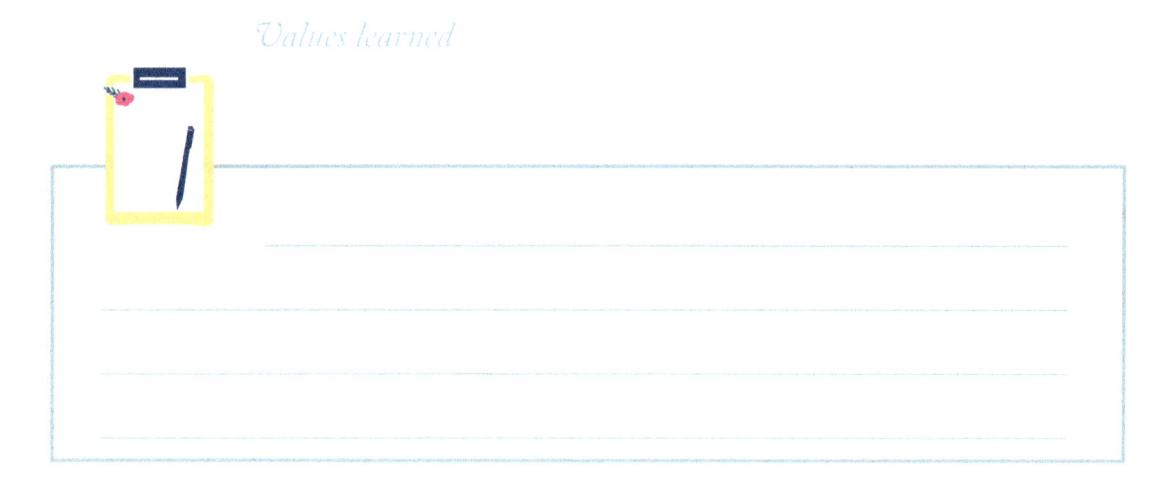

Values learned

Now I Know
- When my plan is set in motion . . .
- When the stage is set . . .
- I accomplish more than imagined.

Now I know

Your Story

Thoughts to Guide Your Thinking

- Look with Eco-Conscious awareness to see what is before you . . .
- Change your thoughts, change your life . . .
- Believe from the depths of your soul, believe with no doubt . . .

As I increase awareness through my senses:

I see

I say

I smell

I feel

I hear

what?

Manifest eco-change.
On to Chapter 4!

4

Clearing the Clutter

REVITALIZE

The essential lesson
I've learned in life
is just to be yourself.
Treasure the magnificent being that you are
and recognize first and foremost
you're not here as a human being only.

You're a spiritual being having a human experience.

Wayne Dyer

My Story
A Clutter Feeling

There is no recollection of a formal introduction to the word "clutter." It was not in my vocabulary as a child and young adult. I believe the phrase of choice was "such a mess." Every piece of clothing, furniture item, accessory, gadget, and plaything in our home was purchased for a purpose and appointed to a special place. To put this into perspective, our junk drawer was organized!

In recent years the phrase "such a mess" mindlessly transitioned into the word "clutter." I view clutter in two forms—physical (what we see) and internal (emotions: what we think, feel, believe)—and have coined the phrase "clutter feeling."

A clutter feeling is the opposite of "Oola" (awesomeness, per The Oola Guys). It is expressed externally by untidiness in the physical space and internally by dis-ease—a state of not feeling at ease on an emotional level. When one or a cluster of clutter situations is on the rise, a mood shift takes place. As a result, feelings of annoyance, anxiousness, distractibility, and forgetfulness are set in motion. None of these emotions reflect a healthy living lifestyle.

The Physical Space—The Cabinet

When I thought of the word clutter, the first pop-up bubble that came to mind was an organized mess. Too much of a good thing, and one item in the wrong place converts into too much stuff, causing a clutter feeling. Imagine entering a bathroom, only to notice the appointments a bit over the top and out of scale.

Recently, a clutter feeling surfaced from the placement of one piece of furniture in my bathroom. The quirky, free-standing mirrored chest with five small drawers stood inbetween the sunken tub and double vanity. As a result, performing a simple task at the sink felt unbalanced. Quite often, my one elbow felt the impact. My sparkle slowly turned into displeasure. One morning I decided—no more! With zest, I glided the chest across the floor and placed it against the wall on the other side of the tub. Clutter free.

The Internal Emotion—The Car

One day while driving my Audi TT between the hills of Chester County, I felt a clutter feeling surface from excess emphasis on "stuff" causing emotional strain. I acknowledged the unsettling feeling and prepared myself to set it free with an empowering little ritual.

Ritual ready, I lowered the window. Lifting my closed left hand to the left side of my temple, I visualized releasing woe thoughts from my mind. With a counterclockwise twist of my wrist, I fully extended my arm out the window and slightly upward. With great power I flicked my fingers open as I verbalized "Swish!" I repeated the action three times.

I reached into my purse to remove the larger of the three Henri Bendel West 57th Satchels in Saffiano leather. Inside sat my trusted on-the-go essential oils. I rhythmically breathed in one of my balancing oils while encouraging uplifting thoughts to complete the emotional shift, thereby entering a state of peace and calm.

Happy thoughts flourished!

Before You Begin

I ask, "What type of mood shift do you experience while in the bathroom?" If the shift is a mood enhancer, a healthy well-being prevails. If your spirit dwindles, why? Does the shift stem from the physical environment, internal, or both? Hence, not feeling your optimum promotes a clutter feeling. Remember, too much of a good thing also causes clutter.

Steps to clearing the clutter are simple, doable even for the novice.

> **clutterlessness**
> **+**
> **organization**
> **=**
> **calm mind**

A Clutter Feeling

Physical Space Clutter

Imagine yourself in the midst of the following scenario. You need to perform a simple task: remove a dangling tag from a dress shirt. You walk directly into the bathroom to the vanity and open the top drawer. Mindlessly you reach into the front left-hand corner next to the tissue box for a pair of scissors. You feel around. A pop-up bubble appears in your mind: *I know I placed the scissors in this very spot.* You push aside the Band-Aid box and tip over the peroxide bottle, making a big mess. You continue with the same approach while rummaging through another drawer. You wonder—who used the scissors last?

As you turn to search inside a cabinet, you notice clothing on the floor and over the shower door. Stuff is everywhere! *Why didn't I notice the clutter before? And where are my scissors? Ugh!*

Internal Clutter

Place yourself in this scenario. You reflect on how the past month was a cycle of over-the-top stressfulness. Finally, relaxation prevails as you anticipate a comfy, restful fullnight's sleep. After snuggling into bed and eventually drifting to sleep you were awakened by your body flip-flopping like a fish out of water. Is it morning? Three a.m.! Eyes wide open. Eventually, you fall back to sleep.

You gasp. Seven a.m.! Did the alarm ring? So much to do in such little time. Distractions build. The phone rings, the phone buzzes, the voice mail alarms—*who needs me, and where are those scissors? I must hurry. Where is my bag? Is that a stain I see?* Back upstairs!

Finally, you're out the door and all is fine. Phew—or is it? That uncomfortable feeling surfaces again. Hmmm, it's a clutter feeling of negative emotions. Thoughts manifest.

The good news: you have control over both environments. Know your triggers. As you become aware of situations bringing forth a clutter feeling, take control before the clutter takes control of you.

The Clearing Goal

Identify the goal by knowing your intention. Pick up your ChaCha bag, and with a slight energy boost, walk to the bathroom. Look around. What do you see? What's popping to cause a clutter feeling? Close your eyes. Visualize the room without the negative pops. Is your energy shifting? Open those gorgeous eyes.

Goal Identifiers

- To designate a place for all necessary products.
- To have only items in the bathroom for this bathroom.
- To create more space within the space; no extra stuff.
- To create an easy transition from the bedroom or hallway to the bathroom.
- To minimize and organize products on open shelves and behind closed doors.
- To feel the joy of a new day without the need to first remove disorganized stuff.
- To learn how to set in motion letting go, letting go . . . of unneeded "stuff."

Goals please

You identified your goal.
You have written your goal.
Take a moment to breathe.
Not too long. We have work to do.

Do not concern yourself with organization at this stage.
The focus for now is to de-clutter.
We will remove the clutter.
We will remove all the "stuff" that no longer serves a purpose.

Be prepared!
You will create a big mess!
A mess is fine. It will not last.
Anything not belonging in this bathroom must go.
Anything causing a cutter feeling must go.

Tools of the Trade

	Release	Renew	Revitalize	
Release	Remain	Relocate	Revitalize	Recycle
	bags	bins	boxes	
	eraser	ruler	straight pins	
	pencil	stapler	tape measure	
		sticky labels		

Clutter

Have you thought about where the source of your clutter comes from each time you enter the bathroom? Are you oblivious to the clutter surrounding you? The key is to identify clutter sources and then to put in place easy, doable solutions for eliminating them. The newfound awareness will guide you to the desired goals with clarity and optimism.

Clutter Sources—The Internal Feeling

Be aware of that pesky internal clutter feeling when your happy self switches to "yuckiness." It may stem from a slip on a towel or bumping into the corner of a drawer to avoid walking over "stuff" on the floor. It may originate from pleasing others by saying yes when you mean no to the wall color, or to the vase on the vanity top that releases negative sentimental energies.

Identify sources

Clearing the Clutter

Three Categories

Design an easy, doable clutter solution for each source. Consciously apply the 3Rs—Release, Renew, Revitalize. Notice the uplifting change taking place within your being.

Release — unhealthy, negative thoughts.

Renew — yourself. Be ritual ready to replace ill thoughts. Reread "My Story: A Clutter Feeling."

Revitalize — with positive uplifting emotions. Sing a little. Dance a little. Laugh a little.

Internal solutions

Clutter Sources—The Physical Space

Be aware of pesky physical space clutter sources clogging up the space. They stem from too much of a good thing, unfinished projects, and pile buildup.

Identify sources

Clutter Solutions—The Tools
The 5Rs are waiting. Get your clutter solution toolbox ready! You will need certain tools for certain projects. How many bags, bins, boxes, and little essentials to gather depends on the amount of clutter to remove. Refer to "The Tools of the Trade" for guidance.

Clear the space.
Clear the mind!

Quick finds in the home

Clutter Solutions—The Physical Space

Five Categories—The 5Rs
Consciously apply the 5Rs—Release, Remain, Relocate, Revitalize, Recycle—to resolve clutter dilemmas. Take note of suggestions and solutions. Once the action-inspiring tasks are set in motion, the uplifting change taking place within you and the bathroom flourishes with ease.

RELEASE
- charitable cause
- children's home
- nursing home
- mom's groups

Have the to-go bag ready!
This step may be a breeze or weighty. Be honest with yourself. If the item no longer serves a purpose, place it in the bag. Label the bag with one of the destinations listed. Let it go! Imagine the joy felt when someone takes ownership of his or her new treasures. Send happy thoughts.

REMAIN
- armoire
- jewelry tray
- little stool
- print (on wall)

Love it!
A perfect complement to this bathroom!
It remains.

RELOCATE
- cleaning items
- vacuum
- light bulbs
- toys

Move to another room!
These items are easily identifiable.
You will know at once to remove and place in another room.

REVITALIZE
- picture frame
- caulk
- chair
- cabinet

Workshop ready?
Can the item be repaired, transformed? If so, does it stay?
Is it best utilized in another room?

RECYCLE/TRASH
- expired
- stained
- cracked
- beyond repair

Nice knowing you.
This category is simple. Look at the item closely.
Is it recyclable or traceable?

102 ••• *Clearing the Clutter*

Clutter Solutions—The Physical Space

Five Categories—The 5Rs
Create easy, doable clutter solutions for each of the 5Rs. Revisit and refresh the list every spring and fall.

RELEASE

REMAIN

RELOCATE

REVITALIZE

RECYCLE/TRASH

Happy 5Rs!

Clear The Path

Be prepared. You are about to create a big organized mess. It's okay. Start with one category and one area at a time. Move clockwise around the bathroom until each section is complete. Action-inspiring steps are listed under The Set Up and grouped into three categories.

Category 1	Items on display
Category 2	Concealed items
Category 3	The questionables

On display items—Essentials are on display, hence can be seen.
Concealed items—Essentials are behind closed doors, hence not seen.

Physical Solutions

The Set Up

Action-Inspiring Steps
1. Gather the 5R tools.
2. Identify each bag, bin, and box with one of the 5Rs. Special note . . .
    Release: Designate a container for each charitable group chosen.
    Recycle/Trash: Designate a container for each recyclable and trash category.
3. Attach labels.
4. Place containers outside the bathroom.
5. Line up one next to the other.

Clearing the Clutter

Category 1—Items on Display

Choose where to begin.

- Identify each item . . .
  - **To go items:** Promptly place in one of the 5Rs containers.
  - **Questionable items:** Place in a separate area, on a flat surface.
  - **Remain items:** Consolidate partially used products. Toss empties.
- Place in proper spot.
- Group like with like.

Category 2—Concealed Items

Choose where to begin.

- Begin with one drawer, one cabinet, and one closet at a time.
- Identify each item . . .
  - **To go items:** Promptly place in one of the 5Rs containers.
  - **Questionable items:** Place in a separate area, on a flat surface.
  - **Remain items:** Consolidate partially used products. Toss empties.
- Place in proper spot.
- Group like with like.

Category 3—The Questionables

Revisit questionable items.

- Make a decision.
  - **Questionable items:** Hold the item and ask yourself, "Does this belong in my bathroom?" Or hold the item and ask yourself, "Will this create a new cycle of clutter?"

Stay on the Clutter-Free Path

Five Keys

Daily

Use a towel, hang it up.
Place soiled clothing in the hamper.
Drop something, pick it up straight away.
Remove shoes, bags, clothing from the bathroom.

Weekly

Perform daily tasks to eliminate weekly clutter buildup!

Monthly

Perform daily and weekly tasks to eliminate monthly clutter buildup!

Spring

Spring is the season for renewal.
Ask yourself: what products need updates to freshen and stay clutter free?

Fall

Fall is the season to release, to let go.
Look for expired "stuff" and let it go.

Daily

Weekly

Monthly

Spring

Fall

Values Learned

- Intuition is key to protect and guide.
- Dab drops of a joyful essential oil and sing to enhance your spirit.
- When decision making is a struggle take a new path.
- Do not second-guess your decision.
- When guilt takes hold, ask yourself why. Let it go. "Swish!"
- No maybe answers allowed, only yes or no.
- Recognize the emotional attachment. Let it go. Continue on.
- Be aware of your sense of accomplishment.
- A clutter-free bathroom = A clutter-free mind.

Values learned

Now I Know

- Like goes with like.
- Consolidate opened bottles, packages.
- When in doubt, set aside until clarity sets in.
- Never place items in a drawer, cabinet, closet, or container temporarily. A big no-no!
- Keep random stuff off the floor.
- Place items in a concealed storage area to prevent a clutter feeling.
- Minimize items on open display.
- Never crowd or overstuff a space.
- Not my style? Let it go.

Now I know

Continue with Chapter 5, "Yin and Yang of Organization," to place items by category, size, and convenience.

Your Story

Thoughts to Guide Your Thinking

- Do you recognize clutter . . .
- How do you resolve internal and physical clutter . . .
- Accomplishments, please . . .

Express a clutter feeling and the feeling of letting it go.

Your path is clear.
On to Chapter 5!

5

Yin and Yang of Organization

HARMONY.....

Always aim at
complete harmony
of thought
and word
and deed.

Always aim at purifying your thoughts
and everything will be well.

Mahatma Gandhi

My Story
The Linen Closet

The organization and tidiness (o&t) of my first bathroom allowed for ease of movement. Unbeknownst to me at the time, a necessary item was missing that would enhance the functionality of the space. The design desperately called for concealed cabinetry.

If I were the interior designer, the plan would have changed ever so slightly to incorporate storage in the bathroom. My proposed approach is as follows:

A narrow linen closet is located on the left-hand side wall, just outside the bathroom. I would remove the closet door, sheet-rock the wall, and embellish with a full-length mirror.

Next up: Increase the square footage of the bathroom by removing the adjoining linen closet. Relocate the toilet to the far wall in the former linen closet. Design a combination on-display and concealed cabinet above the toilet to utilize the space in its entirety.

Last, change the single wall-mounted sink with exposed pipes to a single-sink console with concealed storage beneath. Ta-da! The bathroom revitalization accommodates ample storage in the bathroom to organize products.

In reality, the bathroom never changed.

To this day, I am enamored with Mother's conscious thought process for o&t with purpose in one tiny linen closet. It was a functional organizational system uniquely designed to house products ranging from backup linens to Q-tips on five three-by-four-foot solid oak shelves. Every section grouped and arranged "like with like."

With eyes closed, I recall the uniformity of the linen closet and the fresh, crisp white cotton sheets ironed and folded meticulously. Each set was precisely layered on a shelf, one set on top of the other.

top shelf	linens, blankets
4th shelf	bath towels, hand towels, washcloths
3rd shelf	toilet tissue, tissue boxes, feminine care, cotton balls, Q-tips, curlers
2nd shelf	soap, toothpaste, body cream, baby powder, hair spray, shaving cream
bottom shelf	cleaning agents, light bulbs

Spring, summer, fall, and winter, seven days a week, the linen closet remained the same. No spring or fall cleaning of the closet required.

If I could turn back time, what would I change? The nasty, toxic, synthetic scent of the Zest bath soap and Aqua Net hair spray!

Before You Begin

Are you aware of the energetic shift taking place within you and in the bathroom? Have you noticed the layering effect taking place? You consciously removed toxic substances that were depleting the well-being of a healthy living life force. By clearing the clutter, you acknowledged and let go of shar chi (harmful energy). Transitioning into the next layer of organization will be a breeze. Truth be known, it is already in motion.

Regardless of your personal relationship with style, organization is essential to maintain a harmonious, rhythmic flow. The physical environment is a reflection of inner thoughts. Have you noticed an energetic mood shift while in the bathroom (or the bedroom, or any organized room) versus a room in disarray?

When thoughts are in order, the surroundings reflect a cohesive unity. When a room lacks organizational elements, balance ceases to exist and the joyful mood disappears, as does the desire to be in the space.

With guidance, the process to achieve o&t is easy even for the novice.

o&t
+
calm mind
=
happiness

yin and yang = balance
o = organization
t = tidiness
c = cleanliness

Chi = Energy

Organization enhances well-being, our breathe-able air, and the surrounding physical space. It prevents stagnation and clutter feelings.

You have a choice: to organize or not to organize. When placing yourself in one of the following two scenarios, you will easily recognize when harmonious balance is present or lacking.

Scenario 1

The alarm sings to you for the second time. With eyes wide open, your body remains in the lateral position atop the comfy bed, wishing for ten additional minutes of rest. You feel sluggish, lacking the zing to get hopping up and into the bathroom. You begin to ponder, *Why* do I feel this way? A pop-up bubble appears, taking you through the first phase of morning tasks.

The morning ritual begins with a quick trip to the kitchen to fill a cup with an eye-opening drink. You mindlessly make your way into the bathroom, stepping over a small pile of soiled clothes from the previous day. After placing the energy drink on the sink, you prepare to shower. The warmth of the water feels so good, as does the lathering of fragrant soap and shampoo to awaken the senses. But where is the conditioner?

As your hand feels for where it should be, your eye spots the bottle across the room on the bathtub surround. Ugh! Your drippy body does a quick dash to grasp the bottle, then swiftly returns to the warmth of the shower.

The morning ritual continues with the opening and closing of drawers and cabinets searching for hair, lotions, and oral care products. You take products out, then mindlessly drop, shove, throw, or smush them into a storage area. Finally, you perform a quick once-over, one last glance into the mirror to make certain you are prim and proper. Off goes the light as you exit the bathroom. Fini! Or are you?

Scenario 2

The alarm sings. You are about to rise and shine. However, before hopping from bed you reflect on the previous three mornings of preparing for the day in the bathroom. You begin to ponder, *Why* do I feel light and refreshed with clarity these past few days? A pop-up bubble appears, taking you through the first phase of morning tasks.

A bit sleepy-eyed, you stroll over to the sink, placing a tall glass of room temperature, therapeutic tangerine water on the vanity. The morning routine is set in a fluidity of motion with elimination, oral care, showering, shaving, hair, body and facial care, and dressing your fabulous self.

With each completed task, you unplug plug-ables, return products to their proper storage area, dry all surfaces, hang damp towels, and place soiled clothing in the hamper.

Before flipping off the light switch, you turn and glance to make certain the bathroom is clutter-free, organized, fresh, and sparkly clean. You feel that over-all sense of approval. A smile radiates from within. With a flip of the switch and vigor in your step, you are prepared to take on the day with zest.

Identify Bathroom Chi

A mini chi quiz

- ❏ Do you look forward to the onset of each new day with zing?
- ❏ Do you approach the bathroom with a skip in your step?
- ❏ Is the bathroom organized and tidy?
- ❏ Is it an untidy, disorganized mess from yesterday and the day before?
- ❏ Do you start the day with an artificial energy drink?
- ❏ Do you start the day with a glass of pure, therapeutic water?
- ❏ Do you think to yourself, I *am organized*, only to find when you reach for that "thing," it is somewhere else?
- ❏ Are products arranged with purpose?
- ❏ Do you mindlessly throw "stuff" into a drawer, cabinet, or closet?
- ❏ Do you smush products into a drawer, cabinet, or closet to make them fit?
- ❏ Are the same products stored in more than one location?
- ❏ Do you take notice of all the "stuff" in disarray?
- ❏ Do you think throughout the day about the lack of o&t requiring your attention?

Does lack of o&t in the bathroom extend into other areas of . . .
- ❏ your home?
- ❏ your day?
- ❏ your life?

- ❏ Does the morning ritual cause a clutter feeling?

I encourage you to stand.
Walk, skip, hop, or run to the bathroom.

What do you see?

I ask . . . is this you?

The unconscious regimen
My bathroom is not organized, nor am I. I try to o&t but realize a harmonious, rhythmic flow is lacking. When I breathe in deeply, it's a struggle. I feel . . .
- ❑ a rushing sensation?
- ❑ always searching?
- ❑ irritated?
- ❑ anxious?
- ❑ forgetful?
- ❑ all of the above!

This is my pop-up bubble. Ugh!

Or . . . is this you?

The Eco-Conscious regimen
My bathroom is organized. I transition through the morning routine with ease. When I breathe in deeply, it's a breeze. I feel . . .
- ❑ fresh!
- ❑ clarity!
- ❑ organized!
- ❑ a radiant smile!
- ❑ all of the above!

This is my pop-up bubble. Yeah!

The time is now to feel the energy of uplifting, positive chi!

The Organizational Goal

Identify your goal by knowing your intention. The ultimate goal is to organize with purpose, passion, and a plan. Pick up your ChaCha bag and scooch on over to the bathroom. Look around. What do you see? What's popping to cause o&t disarray?

Close your eyes. Visualize the bathroom without those negative pops. Feel the energetic shift. Open your eyes.

Goal Identifiers

- To consciously enhance the room with proper organizing amenities.
- To open a drawer, cabinet, and closet with a new level of respect and appreciation of the organized order.
- To reach in for the cuticle scissors with ease.
- To forego broken hinges and cabinetry from overstuffing the storage space.
- To eliminate a clutter feeling due to rushing, breakage, and spills.
- To save time, resources, and excess purchases.
- To experience well-being and a positive, energetic connection within the space.
- To love being in the bathroom morning, noon, and night.

Goals please

Goals are enlightening and provide purpose!

The Organizational Approach

Choosing the appropriate staple pieces and on-display and concealed storage to satisfy aesthetics and organization matters. Are you mindful of what, why, where, and how you organize items on display and behind closed doors? Look at the space with a fresh new approach. Envision the possibilities.

Organized Disarray

Does your bathroom reflect organized disarray from lack of clarity concerning storage etiquette—purposeful placement with order?

Imagine opening the vanity cabinet to add additional products. Inside are toilet tissue rolls, hair products, toothpaste boxes, and supplements. Balancing nicely on top is a cotton ball bag, body cream jar, a bath gel bottle, and an accessory bag of goodies. Nothing topples—success!

The reality: order is lacking. It is seen as organized disarray and untidiness. Reach beyond the present arrangement. Take your organizational skills to the next plateau.

**Excess storage props, lack of unity,
oversized cabinets, too many accessories?**

What do you see?

Organization with Purpose

Does your bathroom reflect organization with purpose from consciously thinking about what goes where, why, and how to form balance, unity, and a rhythmic harmonious flow? When these fundamentals are in place, complimentary yin and yang energy manifests.

Imagine for a moment placing Grandmother's three recycled sea-foam glass balloon vases on an open-shelf bookcase. Heartfelt memories begin to tug and swirl while glancing at the sparkles of light emanating from the cluster of crystals beneath the water. The tall flower spikes do a little sway from the opening of the white tuberose blooms. A mindful touch completes the mini composition.

This healthy living ensemble is organized with purpose and naturally becomes a focal point while symbolically uplifting spirits.

Organization with order, organization with purpose, rhythmic flow, unity?

What do you see?

Look at the space once more with a fresh new look.
Envision the possibilities.

Tools of the Trade

O&T Tools

The next step of the journey allows your creative side to awaken and flourish. As the interior decorator it is fruitful to develop clear insight into the organizational process. It's where you become attuned to storage options, present storage, storage solutions, props, products, and DIY props to stay o&t.

Gather Tools of the Trade items—pencil, measure, and camera. Place in your ChaCha bag and then scooch over to the bathroom.

*Organize
with purpose
to stay tidy!*

Storage

Decide what staple and storage pieces stay, what goes, and what you need to purchase. Look at the available floor and wall space when pondering change. Consider changing out a wall sink with exposed pipes for a single sink console with concealed storage. Introduce new, refurbished, inherited, or antique storage pieces or utilize a prop from another room. A functional addition to any size bathroom is a freestanding piece of furniture, such as a chest of drawers or pantry with closed doors that open to a compartmentalized interior.

Things to Think About

storage type	on-display, concealed, combination
permanent	attached, semi-attached, built-in, niche
removable	single-purpose, multipurpose, freestanding
material	wood, slate, wire, glass, textile, stone, ceramic
dimensions	length, width, height
products to store	small (organic cotton balls) to large (fluffy organic bath towels)

On-Display Storage—Options

On-display storage manifests yang (active) energy. Since products are always on visual display, a harmonious balance and tidiness must be present to prevent a clutter feeling.

During the decision process, decide if storage is for a single use or creative versatility. An array of sustainable designs, materials, and finishes are available to complement your personal interior design style story. Do remember that too much of a good thing creates clutter.

Concealed Storage—Options

Concealed storage introduces yin (calm) energy into your personal sanctuary. Visual harmony is projected as your eyes rest on cabinetry similar in design, proportion, and finishes. In addition to the visual beauty, large-scale storage satisfies an array of organizational needs. Selections may include a wall cabinet, vanity, bookcase with bottom doors, sliding doors, soju screens, curtains, freestanding furniture, an ottoman, built-in seating, or any combination.

A comfy, cushioned storage cube and storage window seat are two favorites to complement minimal space and a versatile lifestyle. Either one is desirable to plop a tush and buff ten little toenails, or chitchat with a special someone. Add treasures to the inside, such as a child's favorite blanket or special toy. Or properly store extra linens, bath towels, guest towels, and bath cloths. Cover the top in a delicious eco-textile. Add tufting, buttons, and cording.

Be mindful of props inside of concealed cabinetry. Consider design, quality, quantity, and placement of each. This is key to maintain organization and aesthetic value.

One Section at a Time

To prevent a clutter feeling, begin with one section at a time. Identify the staple pieces, current storage props, and storage availability. Utilize the Eco-Reference Checklist—Staple Pieces + Large Storage + Options to Organize at the end of this section to note present and future design features. It's an organizational delight to maintain o&t. What you choose is a reflection of your personal style story.

The Sink

The sink area is the most versatile and utilized space in the bathroom. It's where you take the first glance of your gorgeous morning self to welcome another day, gargle in freshness, insert contacts, nourish skin, trim a whisker, fluff up hair, and so much more. When you organize with conscious purpose, each task flows with ease regardless of space limitations and ample storage space. It is fine to stand on tippy toes for a product as long as it's within your comfort zone of reach.

Revisit your sink composition, current storage availability, and storage options. Does the design satisfy o&t storage needs? Is ease of accessibility present?

Sink Composition	Above the Sink	On the Sink	Beneath the Sink
double vanity	recessed-mounted mirrored medicine cabinet	built-in drawers	concealed cabinetry ♦ drawer(s) ♦ cabinets ♦ open shelves
pedestal sink	surface-mount mirror medicine cabinet	built-in shelves	pedestal
single sink console	wall-mount mirror—no cabinet	tower cabinet	drawer(s)
wall-hung			semi-open front ♦ drawer(s) ♦ on display shelf

Options to Organize

Add permanent storage to the interior vanity closet to store plug-ables.

Add a permanent shelf under a wall-hung sink.

Add removable storage props under a wall-hung sink—baskets, boxes, tins.

Add a recessed concealed wall cabinet to one or both sides of the sink.

The Shower

Staple pieces, props, and showering products are always on display. Take notice of items beyond the glass shower door, glass wall, knee wall, walk-in, or open shower curtain.

Once in the shower, you subliminally notice the essential tools—shower head, handles, faucet—each is a natural part of the showering experience. Out of scale and lack of storage dampens the shower experience and simplicity of the space. A simple resolve is to organize a small central area for maximum efficiency to eliminate a cluttered mess.

Revisit your shower composition, current storage availability, and storage options. Does the design satisfy o&t storage needs? Is ease of accessibility present?

Shower Composition	Closure	Built-In
single shower	glass door	bench
dual shower	wood door	ledge
	shower curtain	niche
	knee wall	shelf/shelves
	walk-in (doorless)	

Options to Organize

Add	a fashionable spin cabinet.
Add	a vertical tension mount shower caddy
Add	one or multiple wall niches to store cleansing products.
Add	a permanent or removable bench inside the shower for transportables.

The Bathtub

Thoughts of the bathtub involve soaking, playtime, relaxation, aromatic scents, a glass of bubbly, music, and nature. Observe the space surrounding the bathtub. What do you see—a window, wall, mirror, fireplace, two butterflies, a built-in cabinet?

Where do you place the essentials—bath gel, candles, mitts, spritz bottles, glasses, and fluffy bath towels? Are they within arms' reach? Are you considering a permanent solution, such as a niche, half-wall, or shelf composition? Will small transportable props—a bathtub caddy, stool, or bench—suffice?

Revisit your bathtub composition, current storage availability, and storage options. Does the design satisfy o&t storage needs? Is ease of accessibility present?

Bathtub Composition	Built-In
drop-in	hooks
freestanding	ledge
soaking	niche
sunken	shelves
	towel bars

Options to Organize

Roll	fluffy bath towels and place in a round hat box or storage basket next to the tub.
Place	a book, exfoliating gloves, and water bottle on an expandable bath caddy.
Hang	bathrobes and bath towels on a decorative tree stand.
Install	vertical or horizontal niches on the tub wall to organize bathing essentials.

The Shower and Bathtub Combo

Simplicity and versatility of organizational props are essential for shower and bathtub combinations. Both arrangements equate to space limitations for people, props, and cleansing products. The key: choose a storage design to suit the space. A single prop such as a shelf or wall caddy may suffice. A niche is a permanent solution for present and future needs. Add one, two, or three horizontally or vertically to the wall of choice. The perfect options await!

Revisit your shower and bathtub composition, current storage availability, and storage options. Does the design satisfy o&t storage needs? Is ease of accessibility present?

Bathing Composition	Closure	Built-In
shower/bathtub	shower curtain	ledge
	shower door(s)	niche
	shower curtain	soap dish
	knee wall	

Options to Organize

Install	an adjustable or stationary wall caddy to organize products.
Install	three eco-hooks for bath towels within arms reach.
Place	essentials on an expandable bath caddy.
Add	a small wooden stool to place fluff and bathing essentials neatly on top.

Yin and Yang of Organization

The Toilet Room

An array of fashionable and functional props readily awaits to suit your fancy for this small and necessary space. The key is to optimize the storage space to eliminate clutter for a peaceful, relaxing environment.

Wall storage fulfills the quest to organize with purpose and ease of accessibility as it frees up floor space, and minimizes accidental mishaps. Look at the space behind, next to, and across from the toilet, and then explore the possibilities.

Revisit your toilet room composition, current storage availability, and storage options. Does the design satisfy o&t storage needs? Is ease of accessibility present?

Toilet Composition	Closure	Mounted
toilet	door	concealed cabinet
bidet	no door	concealed & on-display cabinet
toilet riser		magazine rack
wall-hung toilet		shelf/shelves
urinal		

Options to Organize

Hang	a concealed cabinet with an open shelf above the toilet.
Place	a magazine rack under a window or to either side of the toilet.
Place	a toilet tissue caddy to hold one functional roll and up to three stored rolls to either side of the toilet.
Add	a small decorative table for necessity items.

The Closet

The interior compartments of built-in and free-standing linen closets are addressed equally. The objective is to organize to embellish and maintain balance, unity, and a graceful visual transition while maximizing the usable space.

The built-in linen closet is a valuable asset, adding functionality and aesthetic beauty to any space from the inside out and the outside in. Arrange and store personal necessity favorites from fluffy textiles to bulky items.

Introduce a timeless freestanding linen closet, such as an armoire or pantry with built-in drawers and shelves.

Revisit your closet composition, current storage availability, and storage options. Does the design satisfy o&t storage needs? Is ease of accessibility present?

Closet Composition	Closure	Built-In
freestanding	curtain	drawers
	solid door	hooks
built-in	solid door with mirror	shelves
	no door	drawers

Options to Organize

Change	the built-in linen closet door to a combination mirror-and-wood door to visually expand the space.
Add	an armoire and compartmentalize the interior with fashionable props.
Add	an organizational system to the inside door of the linen closet.
Add	labels in a **splash of color** to interior organizing props.

The Wall

Additional storage options are available to strategically place on the wall to store, organize, and display bathroom essentials.

Revisit wall compositions, current storage availability, and storage options. Does the design satisfy o&t storage needs? Is ease of accessibility present?

Wall Composition	Built-In	Freestanding	Mounted
built-in	bookcase	leaning ladder with tiers	hooks
attached	niche	combination cabinet	multipurpose unit
freestanding	curtain	on-display cabinet	towel bars
lean on wall	recessed shelves	magazine rack	towel rack, warmer
			modular wall unit
			shelf/shelves

Options to Organize

Add	decorative baskets to each ladder tier.
Add	a built-in bookcase with open shelves and concealed cabinets.
Add	a cabinet with compartments, shelves, and hooks to o&t in one central area.
Open	a small wall section to add recessed shelves, one atop the other.

HARMONY ••• 133

Eco-Reference Checklist—
Staple Pieces + Large Storage + Options To Organize

Note present staple piece compositions, on-display, and concealed storage for each location. Pencil in options. Add new items to the list. Update changes.

Happy, Healthy Eco-Shopping!

The Sink

Sink Composition	Above the Sink	On the Sink	Beneath the Sink

The Shower

Shower Composition	**Closure**	**Built-in**	**Small Props**

The Bathtub

Bathtub Composition	**Closure**	**Built-in**	**Small Props**

Shower & Bathtub

Bathing Composition	Closure	Built-in	Small Props

The Toilet

Toilet Composition	Closure	Mounted	Small Props

Yin and Yang of Organization

The Closet

Closet Composition	Freestanding	Built-in	Small Props

The Wall

Wall Composition	Freestanding	Built-in & Mounted	Small Props

A Natural Progression

Essentials Storage Solutions

Staple pieces, on-display, and concealed storage are identified and in place. The next phase is most creative. It's where you set the stage for organizational delight to maintain o&t.

Prepare to create a checklist of categories and list bathroom essentials. Next up: Choose small props and then decide where to store those necessity items. Utilize the Eco-Reference Checklist—Essentials Categories + Lists at the end of the Tools of the Trade section for present and future needs.

Essentials—Categories + Lists

1. Identify essentials categories.
2. Create essentials itemized lists.
3. Select small storage props.
4. Choose the storage area.

Enjoy a snippet to guide you on your way.

Essentials Category	Essentials List	Qty	Storage Prop	Storage Area
Oral Care	essential oils	1	decorative dish	vanity top
	flosser/floss	1/1	decorative box	vanity drawer
	toothbrush	2		vanity top

toothpaste (natural)	2	decorative box	vanity drawer
tongue scraper	1	pouch/ decorative box	vanity drawer
whitening powder	1	decorative box	vanity drawer

Small Props

Paying attention to behind-the-scene and on-display organizing details makes a noteworthy difference in interior cabinets, drawers, closets, shelves, and surfaces.

Introduce containers (props) to store smaller items. Create a common theme based on style, material, texture, pattern, size, and color. For instance, consider porcelain jars with lids, or fashionable storage bowls and trays for on display props. The unity may be a **splash of color**, a pattern, or a shape. The choice of storage props available are entertainingly delightful.

Transformational Eco-Props

The function, style, and cost of props are endless as well as versatile. It's a PP. Visually they pull the bathroom style story together while presenting clean, refined organization. Inspiring compositions manage to capture the essence of a harmonious, rhythmic flow. We simply can't do without them.

Two common categories of props are ready-made and DIY. There is a third. What's my secret? Transformational eco-props. Transform the original purpose of an item into a new function. The process is simple, immediate, and personalized, with little to no additional cost. How? Shift conventional thought patterns into a creative exercise. At your fingertips are a handful of favorite personalized bathroom and half-bath props transformed into a new function from everyday "stuff" around the home. Utilize the Eco-Reference Guide—Transformational Eco-Props at the end of the Tools of the Trade section to add timeless and newly discovered props.

Allow your creative side
to awaken,
to flourish!

Charisse Marei's Transformational Eco-Prop Designs DIY

Bowls	Look for one-of-a-kind coordinating specialty bowls or dishes. *fill with . . . essential oils, bath salts, jewelry, beauty ingredients*
Boxes	Repurpose cosmetic, jewelry, and hat boxes. For unity, gather durable box designs in various sizes from one designer. *fill with . . . cosmetics, hair care, Q-tips, cotton pads and balls, curlers, towels*
Drapery Holdbacks	Repurpose metal or wood drapery holdbacks and tiebacks for an innovative and eco-chic look. Securely fasten to the wall. *hang a . . . bath towel, hand towel, bath brush, drawstring travel bag*
Jars	Repurpose empty glass jars in various sizes and shapes. Store large quantities of smaller items. *fill with . . . ponytail holders, cosmetic sharpeners, mini stones*
Napkin Holders	Repurpose flat napkin holders into an amazing prop. Place small groupings together. *fill with . . . shaving items, essential oils, supplements*
Office Organizers	Transform office trays, bins, and tins into props. Change the color with an eco-friendly paint or wallpaper to coordinate with the bathroom theme. *fill with . . . hair jewels, nail care, oral care, hair care, styling tools*

Pouches	Repurpose jewelry, game, and gift pouches. Place a charger into the soft cloth pouch and tie with a coordinating repurposed ribbon. *fill with . . . toothbrush charger, shaving charger, small charger, hair bands*
Ribbons	Repurpose ribbon from blouses, strapless dresses, presents, decorative bottles, puppy treat bags, and packaging. Select ribbon length and width in proportion to purpose. *tie a . . . pouch, electronic cords—hairdryer, irons, chargers, razor, flosser*
Tins	Repurpose perfume and tea tins. *prop . . . doorstopper, small hair accessories*
Toothbrush Holders	Repurpose toothbrush holders. Neatly store tall, awkward items. *fill with . . . disposable razors, droppers, cosmetic brushes*

Standard Built-in Designs

under-sink caddy
under-sink pullout
concealed drawers
hair appliance organizer

Exploration = Transformation!

Eco-Reference Checklist—Essentials—Categories + Lists

Create a categories-and-list checklist for bathroom essentials. Choose small props and then decide where to store those necessity items. Add new favorites to the list. Update as needed.

Happy, Healthy Eco-Shopping!

Essentials Category	Essentials List	Qty	Storage Prop	Storage Area

Eco-Reference Checklist—Transformational Eco-Props | DIY

Create a mini eco-chic reference guide to list personal favorites to inspire and satisfy cravings. Add new designs that come your way.

Happy Eco-Props!

Values Learned

- A purposeful approach is the pathway to o&t.
- Look at the space once more with a fresh new look.
- Envision the possibilities.
- Pay attention to the details.
- Listen to my inner voice.
- Keep the positive energy flowing!
- Eco-Reference Checklists are valuable tools in my toolbox.
- O&t + happiness = calm mind

Values learned

Now I Know

- Group like with like.
- Know my storage and prop needs.
- Have an ongoing checklist of haves and must-haves.
- Identify what type of storage to place where.
- Utilize existing storage first.
- Transform that "thing" into a DIY eco-prop.
- Smooth ripples in the textile and align those corners with precision.

Now I know

Your Story

Thoughts To Guide Your Thinking

- Changes . . .
- That special "thing" I cherish is . . .
- I recall a familiar aroma when I open a door . . .

Did I always act with purpose and passion?

Harmonious rhythm is flowing.
On to Chapter 6!

6

Breathe-able Eco-Cleaning

JOY

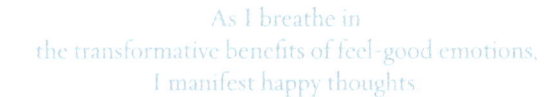

As I breathe in
the transformative benefits of feel-good emotions,
I manifest happy thoughts.

Keep it simple,
stocked, organized, eco, green, clean,
therapeutic, transformational, and plant based.

My Story

Squeaky Clean

I am grateful for two gifts that keep on giving: cleanliness and organization (c&o).

Because I was born into a Roman Catholic family, many beliefs and rituals were instilled. As I sat to write this book, I heard my mother's voice playing over and over in my mind: "God gives everyone special gifts, special talents. If we choose not to recognize and embellish our gifts, He will give your gifts to someone else." As a child, those were pretty scary words. What were my special gifts?

As I reflect on childhood days, there was no aha moment announcing my need for c&o. As a young child, who realizes c&o are gifts anyway? I believe the zeal for c&o began before my first breath of air.

As you read my books, you will discover that c&o are natural complements to each other. Cleanliness = Organization. How can cleanliness be present if there is no order? How can order exist with dirtiness? And if c&o are absent, clutter prevails. In actuality, Cleanliness + Organization = Clutterlessness! My inner self, home environment, and personal "stuff," including the contents of my purse, are all c&o&c (clean and organized and clutterless).

I share with you a glimpse into a segment of an unforgettable childhood memory embedded in my breathe-able clean journey. To multitask while enjoying the simple pleasures in life was invigorating, and bath time was prime time for play, c&o.

Glazed and powdered donuts, oh my! As I carried my cassette player into the bathroom and carefully placed it on top of the toilet seat cover, I thought, "If only I'd sold one more box of glazed donuts to my grandpop, I would be carrying a new mini TV into the bathroom instead of this cassette recorder!"

Once my finger pressed the play tab, the tunes swirled through the air, embracing my being. With a free-moving hair toss, my gaze shifted upward beyond the skylight to receive radiating energy from the natural sunlight. With one smooth motion, I opened the layers of shower curtain fabric to the right, climbed into the bathtub, and closed the curtains to block the light, separating me from the world. This was my time, "me time."

With much enjoyment, I sudsed my body, the tiled shower walls, and the faucet while dancing and singing to the rhythm of the music. After unplugging the tiny round rubber stopper, I cleaned the soap dish and then pushed the suds, layer by layer, down the drain with bits of water.

By now my teeth were chattering as well as my body, and my fingers were truly purple. I could take no more of the cold. I carefully pulled the fluffy bath towel through a slivered self-made opening to snuggly wrap my body till warmth circulated to every limb. Still in my private little world, I dried and buffed the walls, faucet, inner shower curtain, and tub.

Once I was out again, my skin thanked me for the final step of nourishment as it soaked up the topical body cream. All squeaky clean, dry, and nourished, I carefully stepped onto the mat with a sense of accomplishment. This is how my day—every day—began: c&o&c.

Before You Begin

Keep the action-inspiring energy flowing to embrace the luxuries of an Eco-Conscious Breathe-able home. I will guide you through each stage to easily adapt to breathe-able clean methods. This journey is a process to introduce all things eco: storage room essentials, breathe-able and clean designs and recipes, cleaning techniques, and much more.

The aromatic delights will naturally form an interconnectedness between you and the bathroom. To fully engage in the particulars, plant an inner seed with four ingredients—

joy

inspiration

clarity

staying power

to blossom along the way. All of which I believe shine within.

Terms to Guide

Unadulterated[1] pure
synonyms: *absolute *perfect *unalloyed . . .

Distillation[2] the process of purifying a liquid by successive evaporation and condensation.
synonyms: *purify *refine *filter *treat . . .

breathe

c&o = cleanliness & organization
c&o&c = cleanliness + organization = clutterlessness
EO = essential oil
HC = Household Cleaner
NEAT = undiluted

---

1 "Unadulterated." Merriam-Webster.com. Accessed March 23, 2017. https://www.merriam-webster.com/dictionary/unadulterated.
2 "Distillation." Merriam-Webster.com. Accessed March 23, 2017. https://www.merriam-webster.com/dictionary/distillation.

The Key

Picture yourself for a moment, walking into your bathroom.

You've walked these steps countless times before, but today is different. As you approach the transition point (doorway), your spirit is lifted. Your breath of inhalation and exhalation comes with ease and delight. Enveloped in the space is a reflection of bliss emanating from your Eco-Consciousness. You breathe another fulfilling breath of delicious, therapeutic clean air.

You begin to notice fine details in the natural elements that surround you. The tiny bud on the golden pothos plant has soundlessly opened its leaves and is in full splendor, as is the glow of natural sunlight shimmering through the windowpanes as it dances above, through, and around each object in its path.

A subtle glance into the mirror reveals your true inner self radiating with lightness and genuine joy. Unexpectedly, you feel a burst of goose bumps, a symbolic representation of confirmation. You are in your element, a pure, therapeutic, nurturing environment with transformative benefits.

Why are you keenly aware of your breath? Of your surroundings? Of your inner delight? You now hold the key to breathe-able clean within you and within your home.

You willingly uncovered another secret behind a beautiful Eco-Conscious, Healthy-Living Lifestyle.

It all begins with one drop.

One little drop of a pure essential oil. A transformative gift from nature. Imagine yourself immersed in the midst of an organic orange orchard walking on earthy paths of cool, moist, unadulterated soil. The citrus aroma originating from the fruit lures you in. You reach, you grasp, you tug, detaching the orange from the tree as your taste buds do a mouth-watering dance. Spontaneity takes hold as your thumb dips through the fragrant peel separating the rind from the juicy membrane. A spritz of zesty fragrance awakens the senses while enveloping your being in its aromatic qualities, the very essence of the plant.

Essential oils are the life force of the plant for they contain an array of vital nutrients. These concentrated aromatic liquids are derived from botanicals—trees, flowers, herbs, roots, and seeds—and are extracted by a process of steam distillation, cold-pressing, or resin-tapping. They are bottled in glass amber bottles as single oils, blends, and oil-infused products. Use aromatically, topically, and internally to naturally enrich well-being—body, mind, and spiritual connection—as well as within the home to truly experience this mindful and healthy journey.

In my private little sanctuary, each new day begins by setting an intention and reciting a mantra. I select an uplifting essential oil to diffuse aromatically and another to dab over my heart chakra to enhance joy. As I breathe in the transformative benefits of feel-good emotions, I manifest happy belief thoughts.

You see . . .
The bathroom is your private mini sanctuary.
Your special place to clean up.
Freshen up. Tidy up with purity.
Sing a little. Dance a little. Rejoice a little.

Embrace my personal bathroom secrets to help meet all your breathe-able bathroom cleaning needs. Choose what you need. No more. No less.

Everything you need is at your fingertips.

Just reach!

Tools of the Trade

Eco-Cleaner Storage

design
durability
function
material
versatility
sustainability

Eco-Cleaner Storage Preparation

A central place to store cleaning essentials is an absolute for c&o&c. You will go through the process with guidance, taking the guesswork out of the equation.

- -

You will have everything you need.
No more.
No less.

- -

When an unexpected cleaning energy burst sets in, you are prepared. Imagine your body in motion as you walk, skip, run, or hop to the eco-storage area to gather up personalized breathe-able cleaning products. You proudly reach inside a small prop for an organic cotton cloth and an all-purpose botanical cleaner to wipe away a mishap or engage in one-room-at-a-time cleaning.

By chapter's end these three doable steps will be set in motion!

Step 1 Eco-Cleaner Storage	Designate a main storage location—laundry room, mud room, hallway closet, basement, or garage. *Storage essentials:* eco-cleaning materials—equipment, tools, products. Select props to satisfy o&t. *Storage essentials:* on-display, concealed storage, freestanding rack, shelves, baskets, and hooks.
Step 2 Make a Decision	What Tools of the Trade will you choose for daily, weekly, monthly tasks, and for semiannual deep cleaning? Various options are provided to ease the selection process—resources, PPs, tips, ready-made, DIY, and more. Your selections are a reflection of your personal cleaning style. Consider brand, dimensions, material, organic, versatility, texture, pattern, style, and color. Have fun with the process.
Step 3 Gather & Purchase	Check inventory prior to purchasing new products. This valuable step saves time, resources, surplus of inventory, and a clutter feeling. Gone are the days of last-minute running to the store for _____!

Eco-Cleaner Storage Area

The storage area is as unique as your personal style and will vary in design from minimal to complex. Prepare to engage in hands-on projects to create a fully functional eco-storage system. Once in place, maintaining o&t will be a breeze, and the potential for clutter will melt away.

- Measure the available space.
- Choose storage options from each category.

Eco-Cleaner Storage Options

Concealed Storage
Store cleaning products behind closed doors for aesthetic appeal.
- Built-in closet
- Freestanding furniture
- Pre-fabricated closet
- Under-the-sink cabinet
- Wall-hung cabinet

Open Storage
Store cleaning products openly through creative expression and unity.
- Adjustable two, three, or four-tier
- Doorless cabinetry
- Shelving racks
- Wall-mounted shelving

Container (Props)
Design an organizational system. Consider one style in various sizes. Select one or two colors. Add a removable liner in the same textile and color. Label each container with contents (optional). Place the largest containers on the bottom shelf. Use:
- baskets
- boxes
- containers
- liners

Transportable Eco-Storage

Transport small cleaning essentials with ease from the eco-storage area to each floor level, outdoors, and into the trunk of your vehicle. Two options await and fulfill the quest for transportable versatility, o&t, and ease.

ChaCha Bag

Organize the interior with soft goods—apron, cleaning cloths, pouches, and a bottle of water.
   PP: ChaCha bag

Caddy

Organize bottles and cleaning tools.
   PP: Bright bin

Create an eco-storage area using wall space, floor space, cabinet space.

What's your eco-storage?

Eco-Reference Guide + Checklist—Package Label Keywords

Refer to the mini eco-key word reference guide while shopping for Tools of the Trade eco-cleaning products. Add new favorites to the list. Your pathway to an Eco-Conscious, breathe-able clean home is well on its way.

Happy, Healthy Eco-Shopping!

Key Words	Labels	Ingredients
100 percent plant & mineral derived	100 percent natural and certified	100 percent pure essential oils
ecologically friendly	biodegradable (three to five days)	earth friendly
environmentally safe	certified organic	eco surfactants
essential oil-infused	compostable	mineral-based sources
improves IAQ	concentrated formulas	organic plant-based
positive environmental impact	full disclosure/specific ingredient information	organic vegetable oils
renewable organic plant	minimal packaging	plant-based surfactants, fragrances, and/or solvents

Breathe-able Eco-Cleaning

Key Words	Labels	Ingredients
sustainable formulation	no precautionary labels	vegetable glycerin
	sustainably packaged	

Material	Enviro Benefits
cellulose (plant-based materials)—natural fibers, bamboo, organic walnut …	100 percent renewable sources
microfiber cleaning cloths	biodegradable
post-consumer content	compostable
recyclable materials	reduces:
reclaimed wood	♦ contamination
unbleached non-GMO cotton	♦ deforestation
	♦ landfill waste
	♦ water wastage
	♦ global warming

Enjoy the process one step at a time, and breathe in transformational delight!

Breathe-able Eco-Cleaning

Eco-Reference Guide—Storage Room Essentials

Refer to this eco-reference guide while stocking storage room essentials. Add new favorites to the checklist. Update changes. Remember to always:

Keep it simple. Keep it stocked. Keep it organized. Keep it clean.

Happy, Healthy Eco-Shopping!

Eco-Specialty Attire

Fashionable—functional—comfy add-ons. A necessity!

ChaCha Apron	Be inspired. Dress the part. **It's coming!** *Eco-storage area . . . hang on specialty hook*
ChaCha Bag	Transportable go-to bag. Specify a second bag for soft cleaning materials—cloths, pouches, apron, and bottle of water. *Eco-storage area . . . hang on specialty hook*
Gloves	Moisturize as you clean. Hydrate and nourish hands, nail beds, and cuticles. Apply moisturizer and drops of an essential oil. Slip on a pair of organic cotton gloves. *Eco-storage area . . . clip a specialty paper clip onto apron pockets*

JOY • • • 163

Eco-Cleaning Supplies

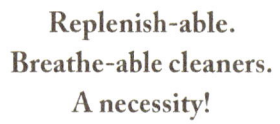

**Replenish-able.
Breathe-able cleaners.
A necessity!**

eco-cleaning tools please

Cleaning Cloths	Repurpose lint-free cotton T-shirts, sheets, pillowcases, and dish cloths. Cut material with fabric scissors into small rectangles and squares. Fold and stack. Place larger cloths on the bottom of the stack. PP: Repurposed T-shirts
Coil Brush	The slender design allows for flexibility to clean depths of interior shower drains. PP: Refrigerator coil cleaning brush *Eco-storage area . . . place in a secondary storage prop*
Containers	Reuse and repurpose eco-friendly storage containers. Consider material, style, stack-ability, and size. PP: *Glass & stainless steel containers with healthy lids* *Eco-storage area . . . place in a secondary storage prop*
Cotton	Choose cotton rounds and cotton balls made from cotton grown on organic farms. A fluffy, versatile, inexpensive tool to satisfy an array of needs. PP: Swisspers 100 percent organic cotton rounds and cotton pads *Eco-storage area . . . place in a secondary storage prop*

Cotton Swabs	A lightweight tool for cleaning small hard to reach areas such as the ribbon. PP: Organyc Beauty wool buds—certified organic cotton and recyclable cardboard stems *Eco-storage area . . . toolbox*
Glass Jars	Recycle glass jars of various sizes and shapes. Adhere a personalized label. Add mixing scrubs. PP: Repurposed round honey glass jars *Eco-storage area . . . place in a secondary storage prop*
Grout Pen	Freshen up discolored grout with one little tool in the perfect color. PP: Grout-Aide grout & tile marker *Eco-storage area . . . place in a secondary storage prop*
Labels	Personalize glass jars and spray bottles. Adhere the appropriate label. PP: Charisse Marei eco-labels *Eco-storage area . . . place in a secondary storage prop*
Plunger	A necessity item to clear toilet blockages. After each use rinse and spritz with HC. Air-dry. Place inside a baggie. Tie with a ribbon or string. PP: Local hardware store *Eco-storage area . . . hang on specialty hook*
Pumice Stone	A non-scratch abrasive pumice stone is the perfect little eco-friendly tool to single-handedly remove toilet bowl ring, hard water, and stains. After each use rinse and spritz with HC. Air-dry. Place inside a baggie. Tie with a ribbon or string. PP: Earthstone Toilet Stone Cleaning Block *Eco-storage area . . . place in a small storage container*

Razor Blade	Easily remove excess paint from windows, vanity top, tile, and floor. Cover blade after each use. PP: Local hardware store *Eco-storage area . . . toolbox*
Sponge	Use a durable eco-sponge for general wipes to intense scrubbing. Choose biodegradable, 100 percent cellulose (plant-based materials) and/or viscos (recycled wood chips), post-consumer recycled materials, sustainably packaged. So many favorites! PP: NatureZway Bamboo Sponge *Eco-storage area . . . place in a small storage container*
Spray Bottle	Glass spray bottles are eco-green! Protect essential oil blends with dark, colored bottles—amber or blue. Choose 8- or 16-ounce bottles for cleaners and 2-, 4-, or 6-ounce bottles for air fresheners, books, and linen sprays. PP: Amber glass spray bottles in various sizes *Eco-storage area . . . place in a secondary storage prop*
Squeegee	Remove excess water and minimize mineral deposit from shower doors, walls, seat, and floor. PP: Frontgate shower squeegee *Eco-storage area . . . in the shower*
Toothbrush	Repurpose retired toothbrushes. This is a forever favorite go-to tool for hard to clean areas, grout lines, drains, and corners. PP: Dental office goodie bag *Eco-storage area . . . place in a secondary storage prop*
Waste Bag	Look for unscented, compostable, non-GMO potato starch, and compostable polymer. PP: If You Care compostable food waste bags *Eco-storage area . . . place in a secondary storage prop*

Eco-Tools

Choose eco-tools by resource, quantity, and size!

Diffuser	An aromatic delight anytime. Consider a portable all-in-one diffuser with on/off timers, output mist control, and requires no water. Attach a 15 ml essential oil bottle to the diffuser. Or drip drops of an essential oil into a water-based diffuser. PP: Young Living *Storage area . . . display on a shelf, table top, or counter*
Diffuser—Book	Delve into mind-enhancing aromatic delight as you read and journal. Spritz the inside pages with Charisse Marei's specialty book spray. It's an eco-chic personal gift of love. PP: Charisse Marei—Breezy Blossom Book Diffuser *Eco-storage area . . . ChaCha bag*
Duster—Floor	Clean the bathroom floor with eco-friendly recycled, renewable, and biodegradable products. Look for an upright scrubber to attach reusable, replaceable floor wipes. PP: NatureZway floor wipes *Eco-storage area . . . hang on hook*
Duster—Wall	Style and functionality! A multi-purpose solution for over-the-top reaches. PP: Frontgate Aluminum Telescoping Duster *Eco-storage area . . . hang on hook*

Stepladder	A safe and sturdy means to clean high, out-of-reach areas—windows, ledges, window dressings, picture frames, chandeliers, and lightbulbs. PP: Frontgate Ultra Slimline two, three, or four-step *Eco-storage area . . . hang on hook*
Vacuum	A quality vacuum is essential. Reduces indoor air pollutants—dust, dust mites, mold spores in the dust, pet hair, and allergens. Choose a vacuum with a HEPA (high-efficiency particulate air) filter and/or a whole-machine HEPA filtration with hygienic bin. PP: Dyson Ball Animal and whole-house central vac *Eco-storage area . . . out-of-the-way location*

Eco-Equipment

Personalize eco-equipment selections with add-on accessories!

Baking Soda	A gentle abrasive cleaner and brightener. Dissolves grease and odor. Pour and store one cup into a small eco-container with lid. Label container. PP: Arm & Hammer Pure Baking Soda *Eco-storage area . . . place in a secondary storage prop*
Castile Soap	100 percent plant based. Pour and store one cup into a small eco-container with lid. Label container. PP: Dr. Bronner's Pure Liquid Castile Soap *Eco-storage area . . . place in a secondary storage prop*

Household Cleaner (HC)	Aromatically delightful, pure botanical-based and oil-infused, antibacterial, antifungal, antiviral. Consider ready-made or DIY. PP: Charisse Marei—DIY HC *Storage area . . . place in each bathroom cabinet*
Distilled White Vinegar	Purifies, cleans, shines, brightens. PP: Spectrum Naturals Organic *Eco-storage area . . . place in a secondary storage prop*
Essential Oils	Choose only pure essential oils. Transformative benefits—aromatically, topically, internally. PP: Young Living *Eco-storage area . . . place in a secondary storage prop, out of direct sunlight*
Lemon Lemon Essential Oil Lemon Juice	A natural cleaner and brightening agent. Dissolves grease, soap scum, mineral organic deposits, oil, and stickiness. PP: All of the above *Eco-storage area . . . refrigerate fresh lemons and lemon juice*
Olive Oil	Cleans and moisturizes. PP: Organic cold pressed olive oil *Eco-storage area . . . place in a secondary storage prop*
Sage	Space clear with a smudge stick or loose leaves to remove negative energy. Smudge before breathe-able cleaning. PP: White sage stick and abalone shell *Eco-storage area . . . place in a secondary storage prop*

Salt	Boosts the effectiveness of baking soda. Pour and store one-quarter cup into an eco-container with lid. PP: Pink Himalayan sea salt *Eco-storage area . . . place in a secondary storage prop*
Vegetable Glycerin	Maintains a creamy paste texture eliminating dry-up in recipes. Love it. PP: Vegetable glycerin (certified organic) *Eco-storage area . . . place in a secondary storage prop*
Vodka	Vodka and witch hazel extends the fragrance time of essential oils. PP: Any inexpensive organic vodka and Hamamelias virginiana witch hazel *Eco-storage area . . . place in a secondary storage prop*
Water	Distilled is the first option, or filtered is the second option. PP: Filtered water *Eco-storage area . . . the kitchen sink*

Eco-Reference Checklist—Storage Room Essentials

Refer to the Eco-Reference Guide—Storage Room Essentials while creating your checklist. Add new favorites to the checklist. Update changes.

Happy, Healthy Eco-Creations!

Eco-Specialty Attire	Qty	Eco-Storage Area
♦ ChaCha Apron		
♦ ChaCha Bag		
♦ Gloves		
♦ _____		
♦ _____		
♦ _____		

Eco-Tools	Qty	Eco-Storage Area
◆ Cleaning Cloths		
◆ Coil Brush		
◆ Containers		
◆ Cotton		
◆ Cotton Swabs		
◆ Glass Jars		
◆ Grout Pen		
◆ Labels		
◆ Plunger		

- ♦ Pumice Stone

- ♦ Razor Blade

- ♦ Sponge

- ♦ Spray Bottle

- ♦ Squeegee

- ♦ Toothbrush

- ♦ Waste Bag

- ♦ _____

- ♦ _____

- ♦ _____

Eco-Equipment	Qty	Eco-Storage Area
◆ Diffuser		
◆ Diffuser—Book		
◆ Duster—Floor		
◆ Duster—Wall		
◆ Stepladder		
◆ Vacuum		
◆		
◆		

Eco-Cleaning Supplies	Qty	Eco-Storage Area
♦ Baking Soda		
♦ Castile Soap		
♦ Household Cleaner (HC)		
♦ Distilled White Vinegar		
♦ Essential Oils		
♦ Lemon		
♦ Lemon Essential Oil		
♦ Lemon Juice		

- Olive Oil

- Sage

- Salt

- Vegetable Glycerin

- Vodka

- Water

-

-

-

Breathe-able Eco-Cleaning

Breathe-able Air

You are now well aware that exposure to synthetics—cleaners, air fresheners, and candles—adversely affects physical and emotional well-being, IAQ, and the natural outdoor environment. Allow me to share a repetitive reaction when my senses detect synthetics in a bathroom.

My body stiffens.
My eyes widen.
My shoulders do a little shake as I gasp.
Do I breathe in?
Hold my breath?
Do a turnaround and exit?
But!
Ugh!
What is an au naturel gal to do?

Scrunch a bunch of toilet tissue and press against my nose—tinkle, wash, and run!

My wish is for you to say bye-bye to all harmful chemical-laden products including the all-to-familiar air fresheners—shelf and countertop designs, plug-ins, sprays, along with petroleum-based fragrant candles. Prepare to readily replace with my healthy timeless options. They are creatively simple and interchangeable.

Breathe-able Eco-Cleaning

Eco-Designs + Recipes

JOY

Eco-Conscious Design + Recipe Benefits

love
refreshing
few ingredients
a gift from nature
more closet space
a touch of pure love
a conversation piece
aromatically delicious
huge monetary savings
a burst of sweet sunshine
antibacterial, antifungal, antiviral
boosts the effectiveness of the clean
breathe-able plethora of delicious air
versatility and simplicity are abundant
purifies the air to transformational clean
friendly to you, me, children, furry friends, our Earth
your journey to a beautiful Eco-Conscious, Healthy-Living Lifestyle
share
share
share

Charisse Marei's Eco-Air Freshener Designs DIY

DIY Recipes to follow!

Air Vent	Place a small organic cotton ball or cotton pad just inside the vent. Add a favorite single or blend of a pure essential oil.
Breathe-able Air Sprays	Spritz the air throughout the day with Charisse Marei's breathe-able air sprays.
Decorative Bowl	Place a special small decorative bowl containing mini gemstone chips on a shelf or by the bathtub. Add two drops of an essential oil. Toss gently. Refresh as needed.
Diffuser	Diffuse to disperse tiny molecular particulates into the air to cleanse, purify, and freshen the air. Choose a small portable diffuser to place on a shelf or vanity top.
Drawers + Linen Closets	Personalize the interior. Line with sustainable wallpaper. Repurpose small jewelry boxes, jewelry pouches, and organic muslin bags. Up the design with a monogram, ribbon, buttons, or jewels. Fill recipe on page 192.

Pouch + bag options...

- Place in several drawers.
- Gently lay on a shelf.
- Gently lay on a top stack of clean towels.
- Hang from a hook.

Essential Oils	Pure essential oils are authentic and faithfully aromatic, delivering superlative eco-delight. Add single drops or blends to props and to diffuse the air. Opt for a new essential oil each month. PP: Bergamot, lime, orange, rosemary, thyme
Hamper	Place a mini sachet or muslin bag inside the hamper or adhere to the inner lid. For continuous aromatic delight, add several drops of an essential oil to the inside contents each morning. *Adhere options . . . decorative safety pin, ribbon, velcro*
Plants	Place three mini stones and a drop of essential oil into the soil. Spritz leaves with one of Charisse Marei's breathe-able air fresheners or linen sprays.
Reading Material	Spritz the interior pages of magazines, books, coloring books, and reference material with Charisse Marei's Breezy Blossom Book Spray.
Tissue Box and Tissue Cover	Add a drop or two of an essential oil to an organic cotton pad or refill pad. Adhere behind the box or to the inner cover. Spritz the tissue box with one of Charisse Marei's breathe-able air fresheners or linen sprays. *Adhere options . . . double face tape*
Toilet Tank	Spritz the inner lid. Add a drop or two of an essential oil to a cotton refill pad and place behind the tank. *Adhere options . . . double face tape*
Toilet Tissue Roll	Spritz the roll. Drip a drop of an essential oil inside the roll, or spritz with one of Charisse Marei's breathe-able air fresheners or linen sprays.
Towels	Spritz bath and hand towels before and after each use.

Vacuum	Lightly fill a muslin bag with organic cotton balls. Drip several drops of an essential oil directly to the cotton. Tie the bag. Place inside the vacuum.
Wastebasket	Drip two drops of an essential oil onto a small organic cotton ball or cotton refill pad. Place inside the wastebasket. Keep waste tidy with a reusable disposable liner (optional). *Adhere options . . . double face tape*

Happy, Healthy DIY Eco-Creations!

Eco-Reference Guide + Checklist— Eco-Air Freshener Designs

Refer to Charisse Marei's Eco-Air Freshener Designs to create personal eco-creations. Note personal favorites to inspire and satisfy cravings. Add new designs that come your way. Revisit often.

Happy, Healthy Eco-Shopping!

Design Placement	Eco-Air Freshener Designs

Charisse Marei's Breathe-able Cleaning Recipes + How-To's DIY

Before You Begin Tips

Ingredients	Organic, fresh, and pure, please.
Bottles	When adding essential oils to a recipe opt for dark glass bottles—amber or cobalt blue.
Mini-Bottle Blends	Add ingredients to a 16-ounce bottle, shake. Pour into 2-, 4-, or 6 ounce bottles.
Intensify	Add extra drops of essential oil to increase aromatics.
Essential Oils	Switch out an essential oil to satisfy your PP.
Distilled vs. Filtered Water	It's a PP. My PP is filtered.
Vodka vs. Witch Hazel	It's a PP. My PP is vodka even though I do not consume alcohol.
Time	Allow each freshly made blend to sit for ten-ish minutes before tweaking to your delight.
Action-Inspiring	*shake * spray * sniff*!
Final Touch	Be label ready.
A Glance	1 ounce = 1/8 cup = 2 tablespoons
The Recipe	Gather, blend, and manifest with pure love.
How-To's	Enjoy the what, where, and how-to section after each recipe.

BREEZY BLOSSOM BOOK SPRAY

Give books life with ingredients inspired by nature. Spritz with rhythmic joy. Breathe in deep breaths, release, and breathe in some more botanical delight.

Gather	Blend	Manifest
Four 2-ounce glass spray bottles	essential oils:	inner love
labels	8 drops each bergamot, rosemary	
measuring tools	5 drops each lavender, orange	
	1 ounce vodka	
	2 cups filtered water	
	*add * shake * sniff*	

SPRITZ

WHERE

books   magazines

LET'S DO IT
Spritz books while in the toilet room, in bed, on a chair.
Spritz books while traveling on an airplane, in a train, on a boat.
Spritz books while in a cafe, on a blanket, sitting on a wall.
*shake * spritz * sniff*

SWEET VISIONS LINEN SPRAY

Refresh the senses with ingredients inspired by nature to nurture a consciously green sense of well-being. Place a linen spray bottle in each bathroom next to the Burst of Sunshine Air Freshener bottle, for in reality they are interchangeable. Refill as needed.

Gather	**Blend**	**Manifest**
Two 4-ounce glass spray bottles	essential oils:	enchantment
labels	10 drops lavender	
measuring tools	8 drops orange	
	4 drops ylang-ylang or geranium	
	1 ounce vodka	
	top off with distilled water	
	*add * shake * sniff*	

SPRITZ

WHERE

linens   throws   towels

LET'S DO IT

Spritz linens after folding, in the closet, on a shelf, in a drawer, on a bed, pillows, too.
Spritz throws after folding, in the closet, on a shelf, in a drawer, over your body.
Spritz towels before a beauty ritual, in the closet, on a shelf, on a hook.
*shake * spritz * sniff*

Breathe-able Eco-Cleaning

BURST OF SUNSHINE AIR FRESHENER

Choose a spray to heighten your senses and to empower an aromatic day of bliss. Place an air freshener spray bottle in each bathroom next to the Sweet Visions linen spray bottle, for in reality they are interchangeable. Refill as needed.

Gather	Blend	Manifest
Two 4-ounce glass spray bottles	essential oils:	happy chi
labels	12 drops orange	
measuring tools	6 drops each lemon, lime	
	4 drops each citrus fresh, grapefruit	
	3 drops peppermint	
	1 ounce vodka	
	top off with filtered water	
	*add * shake * sniff*	

SPRITZ

WHERE

air	bath mats	drawer liners
plants	reading material	tissues
toilet bowl	toilet tissue	

LET'S DO IT

Spritz to eliminate odor.
Spritz to enhance freshness.
Spritz to promote life.
Spritz to increase the splendor of the day.
*shake * spritz * sniff*

ESSENTIAL OIL AIR FRESHENER

Heighten the scent of the bathroom and half bath all day. Drip drops of a favored essential oil (citrusy, floral, minty) straight from the bottle and onto small props: gem stones, cotton, sachet & bag.

Gather	Blend	Manifest
2 mm multicolored gemstones	essential oils:	uplifting emotion
3 small garden stones	2 drops lavender	
3 mini rose buds	6 drops rosemary	
small decorative bowl	*add * mix * sniff*	

GEM STONES

WHERE

shelf   tub surround   vanity

LET'S DO IT

Drip drops onto a mini composition to inspire the senses.
Drip drops add stones and essential oil to the bowl. Swish in a circular motion.
Drip drops switch out the garden stones for rose buds from your fresh flower arrangement.
*drip * swish * sniff*

Breathe-able Eco-Cleaning

COTTON

Gather	**Blend**
cotton ball/pad	2 drops essential oil (PP)
cotton scent pad	

WHERE

air   hamper   tissue box

toilet tank   toilet tissue roll   vent

wastebasket

LET'S DO IT
Drip drops on to a cotton prop. Add suggested essential oils or mindfully drip drops of a favored essential oil onto the cotton. Place or adhere to location.

*drip * place * refresh*

SACHET & BAG

Gather	**Blend**
2 mm gemstone chips	essential oils:
2 inch sachets	3 drops each jasmine, lavender
cotton pads	dried herbs
small muslin bags	dried flowers
	wood chips
	*add * mix * sniff*

WHERE

closet	drawer
linen bag	linen closet

LET'S DO IT

Fill sachets or bags with a combination of gemstones, flowers, herbs, and wood chips.
Drip drops directly onto a cotton pad and insert into the sachet or muslin bag.
Refresh and replace the cotton pad as needed.

*add * place * refresh*

Breathe-able Eco-Cleaning

DIFFUSE TO PURIFY

Diffuse daily, in the a.m., p.m., or inbetween to purify and rid of germs, unpleasant odors, negative energy, and under-the-weather blues.

Gather	Blend	Manifest
2 mm multicolored gemstones	essential oils:	inner breath
diffuser	16 drops each clove, lemon, orange	
glass bottle dropper	6 drops rosemary	
label	10 drops each cinnamon, rosemary, tea tree	
small muslin bags	*add,* diffuse * breathe*	

DIFFUSE

WHERE
air

LET'S DO IT
Diffuse place the diffuser in the lower, main, or upper level to purify the air.
Diffuse add blend to the diffuser of choice.
*ready * set * breathe*

HOUSEHOLD CLEANER (HC)

This formula delivers natural derived ingredients for a powerfully purifying and aromatically delightful eco-clean. Rest at ease as children and furry friends crawl, play, and lick those toys with zest.

Gather	Blend	Manifest
16 ounce glass spray bottle	essential oils:	delicious clean
label	12 drops each clove, lemon, eucalyptus	
measuring tools	8 drops each cinnamon, rosemary	
	1/3 cup distilled white vinegar	
	1/3 cup distilled white vinegar	
	top off with warm filtered water	
	add, shake * go*	

SPRITZ

Gather		Manifest
buffing + spritz cloth	HC	sparkle + shine

CLEAN

bathtub	cabinetry	floor	handles & knobs
shelves	shower	sink	stains
tile	toilet seat		

LET'S DO IT

Spritz the cloth and wipe to clean.   **Flip** the cloth over to buff.
*shake * spritz * wipe*

Breathe-able Eco-Cleaning

WASH

Gather

| comb | hand towels | toothbrush |
| HC | | |

CLEAN

body brushes · cosmetic brushes · cosmetic sponges

exfoliating gloves · exfoliating mitts · hair brushes

LET'S DO IT
Strip brushes of hair. Hold hair brushes over wastebasket and remove hair with a comb.
Fill the sink with tepid water and a splash of HC.
Wash between hairbrush bristles with a toothbrush. Squish, rub, and squeeze other products until clean. Rinse. Air-dry on the hand towel.
*soak * wash * dry*

SPARKLE + SHINE GLASS CLEANER
Take deep breaths while formulating the citrus blend of green clean.

Gather	**Blend**	**Manifest**
16 ounce glass spray bottle	essential oils:	cheerfulness
label	16 drops lemon	
measuring tools	8 drops each lavender, orange	
	1 cup distilled white vinegar	
	1/4 teaspoon pure castile soap	
	top off with tepid filtered water	
	add, * *shake* * *go*	

SPRITZ

Gather		
buffing cloth	spritz cloth	Sparkle + Shine Glass Cleaner

CLEAN

beads	chandeliers	compacts	crystals
faucets	glass frames	jars	lightbulbs
light fixtures	mirrors	windows	shower door

LET'S DO IT
Spritz the cloth. Wipe to remove smudges. Flip the cloth over, buff. Or use two cloths. One hand wipes and the other buffs.

shake * *spritz* * *wipe*

Breathe-able Eco-Cleaning

CREAMY GRIT SPECIALTY SCRUB + A TWIST OF FENG SHUI

This delightfully aromatic scrub is so powerful that it's anti-everything as it removes grimy build up, brightens, and shines. It's your new go-to jar. Double and quadruple the recipe and "gift" to loved ones with purpose. Refer to subsections on where and how to clean: drains + jets, mold + mildew, and rings.

Gather	Blend	Manifest
8 ounce lidded glass jar	essential oils:	confidence
bowl	20 drops lemon	
label	8 drops each tea tree, thyme	
measuring tools	1/4 teaspoon fresh thyme leaves (see steps)	
small flat wooden spoon	4 teaspoons vegetable glycerin	
	1 cup pure baking soda	
	2 pinches sea salt	
	2 teaspoons pure castile soap	
	±1/4 cup filtered water	
	add, * *mix* * *go*	

THE STEPS
1. Dry out fresh thyme completely.
2. Pinch off a tiny sprig, set aside.
3. Detach leaves from stem. Sprinkle a few leaves into the bottom of jar.
4. Add ingredients to the bowl. Gently stir to a slight creamy texture. Spoon into jar.
5. Garnish with sprig.
6. Attach label to jar.

The Twist

Visualize your intention as you sprinkle leaves on bottom of jar.
Add a pinch of this and a drop of that.
With a wooden spoon, stir the mixture in clockwise motion.
As you stir, say your intention out loud.
Spoon mixture into jar.
Place sprig atop.

believe

RUB

Gather

buffing cloth	Creamy Grit Specialty Scrub	hors d'oeuvre knife
cleaning cloth	HC	toothbrush

CLEAN

bathtub	caulk	chrome	covers
drains	faucets	floors	mold
shower walls	sinks	stains	tile
toilet bowls			

LET'S DO IT

Dip the knife into the jar.
Add a dab to the cloth and toothbrush and clean away.
Spritz with HC.
*scrub * rinse * buff*

DRAINS + JETS

Gather

buffing + cleaning cloth	toothbrush	Creamy Grit Specialty Scrub
long-handle brush	Q-tip	HC
small brush		

CLEAN

bathtub jets   drains—bathtub, shower, sink   sink air hole

LET'S DO IT
Scrub the inside and outer surface of drains to remove buildup. Finish up with a spritz of HC, buff.

Scrub bathtub drain and jets with grit, brushes and Q-tips. Finish up with a spritz of HC, buff.

*scrub * rinse * buff*

MOLD + MILDEW

Gather

buffing cloth	toothbrush	Creamy Grit Specialty Scrub
cleaning cloth	long-handle brush	HC
small brush	Q-tip	

CLEAN

drains—bathtub, shower, sink	drywall—surface
grout—shower, corners, floor	shower—track, frame, glass
sinks—caulk, faucets	windows—corners, track, trim

LET'S DO IT
Spritz with HC and let sit for ten minutes. Do not rinse.
Scrub add Creamy Grit to the area. Scrub inside and outer surfaces. Repeat as needed.
*spritz * scrub * rinse*

RINGS

Gather

buffing + cleaning cloth	essential oils:	Creamy Grit Specialty Scrub
cleaning gloves	4 drops pine, citrus fresh, or	HC
pumice stone	lavender (pick one)	
toilet bowl brush		

CLEAN

bidet   toilet bowl   urinal

LET'S DO IT

Rings use the pumice stone to remove stains.
Inside add Creamy Grit to the bowl, scrub, and flush. Add drops of essential oil to freshen. Let sit.
Outside add Creamy Grit to the damp cloth to remove marks and clean surfaces. Spritz HC.
*scrub * flush * buff*

LET IT SHINE WOOD POLISH

Take notice of the lustrous shine gleaming from wood surfaces with this *au naturel* polish. Go ahead and breathe in fresh aromatic purity.

Gather

4 ounce spray or pour bottle

labels

measuring tools

Blend

essential oils:

15 drops each lemon, orange

6 drops bergamot

3 tablespoons organic olive oil

1 1/4 cup distilled white vinegar

add * *shake* * *sniff*

Manifest

uplifting flow

GLIDE

Gather

buffing + spritz cloth

CLEAN
wood surfaces

LET'S DO IT
Add a small amount onto the cloth.
Dab the cloth together to even out the liquid.
Tuck fingertips inside the cloth to clean corners. Flip the cloth.
Buff in circular motions. A little bit goes a long way.
shake * *spritz* * *buff*

FLOORING FLUFF

Boost the clean to freshen and brighten fluff stuff with this eco-friendly formula. Your furry friends will wag their tails with joy.

Gather	Blend	Manifest
small lidded container	essential oils:	thoughtfulness
spoon	10 drops lemon	
measuring tools	1/4 teaspoon Pink Himalayan Sea Salt	
	*add, * shake * stir*	

SPRINKLE

CLEAN

area rugs	bath mats	fluff
furry friends beds	non-slip pads	

LET'S DO IT

Sprinkle onto fluff stuff. Let sit for thirty-ish minutes. Vacuum. Place in the natural sunshine for an extra whitening boost. Return and spritz with a Burst of Sunshine Air Freshener.
*sprinkle * sit * shake*

FLOORING

Minimize eco-cleaning products. Clean floors with one product: HC. The question is, will you choose the duster or cloth?

WASH

Gather

cleaning cloth • floor duster • HC

CLEAN

hardwood   stone   tile

LET'S DO IT
Spritz small sections of the floor with HC. Clean with cloth or floor duster. Begin at the furthermost area, finishing at the doorway.

*spritz * glide * buff*

*You
move a little . . . wiggle a little!*

Prevention—Be Proactive

LITTLE CRITTERS & INSECTS—THE EXTERIOR
This blend protects life. Formulate with heartfelt thoughts.

Gather	Blend	Manifest
label	essential oils:	peaceful chi
lidded container	8 drops each lemon, peppermint, rosemary	
measuring tools	1/2 cup baking soda	
	1/2 cup powdered sugar	
	*add, * shake * stir*	

SPRINKLE

CLEAN

cracks   follow the trail   perimeter of house

LET'S DO IT
Shake and sprinkle around the perimeter. Repeat as needed and after each rainfall.
Inspect the perimeter. Seal cracks and holes.
Plant basil, mint, peppermint, thyme, and/or lavender plants outside and near the point of entry.
*mix * sprinkle * repeat*

LITTLE CRITTERS & INSECTS—THE INTEROR

This blend protects life. Formulate with heartfelt thoughts.

Gather	Blend	Manifest
4 ounce spray bottle	essential oils:	peaceful chi
label	10 drops each of peppermint, rosemary	
mini cotton ball	filtered water	
mini oil dish		
	add*blend*sniff	

SPRITZ + DROPS

CLEAN

cracks	drains	floor
stickiness	vanity top	window tracks

LET'S DO IT

Shake bottle add essential oils and water. Spritz sills and drains.
Dish select a softly edged bordered dish. Add essential oils. Place on the vanity.
Oils add droplets of both essential oils to balls and pads. Place on the sill.

shake* spritz* repeat

MOLD & MILDEW

This blend protects. Formulate with heartfelt thoughts.

Gather	**Blend**	**Manifest**
cleaning cloth	Creamy Grit Specialty Scrub	positive emotions
scrubbing brushes	HC	
	shake*shake*shake	

SCRUB

CLEAN

drains—bathtub, shower, sink	grout—shower, corners, floor
shower—track, frame, glass	windows—corners, track, trim

LET'S DO IT
Scrub weekly to prevent mold. Rinse. Repeat.
Repair leaks promptly.
Replace porous material with new drywall and grout.
sniff* look* act

DIFFUSE

Gather

diffuser   "Diffuse to Purify" Essential Oil

WHERE
air

LET'S DO IT
Ventilate open windows.
Vent install a fully operable exhaust fan and vent to the outdoors.
Diffuse to dissolve potential mold spores with a purification essential oil.
*spritz * glide * buff*

*You
Be happy.
Prevention recipes promote life!*

How To Eco-Clean

JOY

Eco-Clean

Breathe-able cleaning is my forte. It's where I sparkle and shine! I believe you are ready to join me, to be part of my team. Knowing how to clean enriches the task of cleaning. As you learn you will develop a system, form a rhythm, and see progress. This equates to positive chi that synergistically harmonizes within your being and filters through the bathroom.

Where does one begin? At the beginning, of course. Choose the approach: on-the-spot cleaning (SC), thorough cleaning (TC), or in-depth breathe-able clean (IDBC).

The constant is thoroughness.
The variable is the amount of time given.

Spot Cleaning = SC

Wipe up, dry down, buff up as you go. When? After bathing, showering, sink regimens, elimination, and touch-ups. The approach prevents a dirty, messy, smelly buildup of products, clothing, fingerprints, spots, grime, mold, and a clutter feeling.

Thorough Cleaning = TC

More time, more tools required. Each segment of time builds upon the other. Acquire a rhythm and develop a ritual, and the newly learned steps will be a breeze.

In-Depth Breathe-able Cleaning = IDBC

Focus on the details with a keen eye. Apply the TC method with the utmost thoroughness. Little changes equate to a newness, a breath of fresh air.

Daily Freshness
Weekly Freshness
Monthly Freshness
Semi-Annual Freshness

Daily

Be mindful of your space.
Freshly spritz, fluff, and tidy with purity.
Sing to and spritz live, healthy plants.
Do a once-over before exiting.
Release * Renew * Revitalize

Weekly

Consistency is essential.
Perform daily tasks to eliminate weekly grime buildup.
Release * Renew * Revitalize

Monthly

Each month is a new beginning.
Open the windows.
Wash, spritz, and fluff those area rugs.
Release * Renew * Revitalize

Spring

Spring is the season for renewal.
Shift the energy!
Ask yourself, what do I need to change to bring in anew?
Release * Renew * Revitalize

Fall

Fall is the season to let go.
Shift the energy!
Negative thought? Let it go. Expired, broken stuff? Let it go.
Out with the old, in with the new.
Release * Renew * Revitalize

Daily Etiquette + Eco-Freshness
Spot Cleaning = SC
Gentle Reminders

- Look forward to the onset of each task with zing.
- Be mindful of your space.
    - Freshen the air:
    - open a window
    - spritz the air
    - diffuse an essential oil
- Turn the water off while doing a task.
- Tidy up as you go:
    - cap on
    - bottle clean
    - put away
    - wastebasket
- Replace the empty tissue box.
- Replace the empty toilet tissue paper roll.
- If you sprinkle when you tinkle, be certain to clean up.
- Close the toilet seat lid before you flush.
- Wash hands.
- Sink and vanity top: remove, toothpaste, hair, soap, and water spots, dry.
- Hand towel/wash cloth:
    - fold
    - hang
    - hamper
- Remove excess "stuff" from the shower/bathtub.
- Before exiting the shower:
    - dry surfaces
    - close bottles
    - place all products on the shelf
- Remove slippery oils from the standing area in the shower and bathtub.

- Air-dry bath towels:
    - hang on the towel bar
    - hang on a hook
- Hamper: place dirty clothes, cloths, and towels inside, close lid.
- Place all contents in their special storage area.
- Air-dry: washcloths, bath gloves, body brushes.
- Spritz and buff smudges on glass and mirrors.
- Give plants a drink of water.
- Dry and buff wet areas: sink, vanity, shower, shower door, bathtub, floor.
- Unplug all plug-ables!
- Fluff and straighten bath mats and area rugs.
- Shopping list: add low-inventory items to the eco-shopping list.
- Spritz the air.
- Turn off lights.

Daily Etiquette + Eco-Freshness Spot Cleaning = SC Details

Shower/Bathtub	*Two tools: squeegee, hand towel* After showering, use the squeegee to remove droplets of water from all surfaces. Tuck fingers in the towel to eliminate moisture in the track. Dry personal products, tile, glass, and shower curtain.
Sink/Vanity Top	*Two tools: HC, cloth/sponge* After each task wipe and place personal care products in the proper storage area. Spritz and buff—sink, vanity top, mirror.
Toilet	*Three tools: HC, cloth/sponge, toilet bowl brush, essential oil* Spritz, swish, flush, and rinse the brush clean. Drip in drops of essential oil.

JOY

Walls & Switch Plates + Doors & Knobs	*Three tools: HC, cleaning cloth, essential oil* Spritz cloth with HC. Gently wipe away grime.
Mirrors, Glass, + Windows	*Two tools: Sparkle glass cleaner, cloth* Be gone, noticeable smudges. Spritz cloth, wipe, and buff.
Trash	*One pair of hands* Pick up empties, paper, and lint. Place in wastebasket to prevent messy buildup.
Floor	*Two tools: HC, cloth* Spritz spots on floor and wipe.

Weekly Eco-Freshness
Light Breathe-able Cleaning
Gentle Reminders

- Look forward to the onset of each task with zing.
- Be mindful of your space.
    - Freshen the air:
    - open a window
    - spritz the air
    - diffuse an essential oil
- Air fresheners:
    - refresh cotton balls, pads, and refill pads
    - muslin bags
    - sachets
- Tidy up: place all contents in their special storage area.
- Toilet and bowl: clean inside and out. Close the toilet seat lid.
    - Toilet tissue holder:
    - add a new roll to holder
    - fill stand
    - fold under ends to make a point
- Sink: remove toothpaste, hair, soap. Clean and buff.
- Mirrors and glass: spritz and buff away smears.
- Vanity: clear clutter, spritz, clean, buff.
- Shower and bathtub:
    - remove toys, cloths, accessories
    - close open bottles, place on shelf
- Soiled bath and hand towels:
    - wash
    - fold (align corners to fold)
    - return to special storage area
- Hamper: remove soiled articles, place in laundry room.
- Air-dry washcloths, bath gloves, and body brushes.

- Walls, plates, doors, knobs: spritz smudges, wipe.
- Wastebasket: empty, spritz, wipe. Replace eco-air freshener and specialty bag.
- Feed the plants: spritz with eco-air freshener.
- Floor: wipe and buff.
- Bath mats and area rugs: shake outdoors, wash, air-dry, replace.
- Release, Renew, Revitalize DIY eco-air fresheners.
- Unplug all plug-ables!
- Shopping list: add low-inventory items to the eco-shopping list.
- Spritz the air.
- Turn off lights.

Weekly Eco-Freshness
Light Breathe-able Cleaning
Details

Shower/ Bathtub	*Four tools: HC, Creamy Grit, cleaning & buffing cloths* Remove loose items. Spritz HC on all surfaces including the inner shower curtain. Let sit for ten minutes. Clean all tub and shower surfaces with Creamy Grit, rinse. Tuck fingers in the cloth to thoroughly dry corners, drains, and track. Dry loose items. Return to proper storage.
Sink/Vanity Top	*Four tools: HC, Creamy Grit, cleaning & buffing cloths* Remove loose items. Clean area with Creamy Grit and cloth, rinse. Spritz HC, wipe, and buff. Spritz and dry loose items, one at a time. Return to vanity top.
Toilet	*Five tools: HC, pumice stone or toilet brush, cleaning cloths, gloves, essential oil* Gather gloves and the pumice stone to remove toilet bowl stains. For general cleaning spritz all areas with HC. For extra brightening add Creamy Grit and brush away. Be certain to scrub under the rim. Wipe and buff surfaces. Add an essential oil to the toilet bowl water. Do not flush.

Toilet Tissue Holder	*Three tools: HC, cleaning cloth, essential oil* Spritz cloth, wipe, and refill toilet tissue and essential oil.
Walls & Switch Plates + Doors & Knobs	*Three tools: HC, cleaning cloth, essential oil* Spritz cloth with HC, wipe, buff. Remove crayon and stickiness with lemon or lime essential oil.
Mirrors, Glass, Windows, + Light Fixture	*Two tools: Sparkle glass cleaner, cloth* Be gone, noticeable smudges. Spritz cloth, wipe, and buff.
Trash	*One pair of hands* Discard trash. Spritz HC over entire waste basket, wipe, buff. Add a fresh-scent eco-air freshener to inside bottom. Add trash bag.
Floor	*Two tools: HC, cloth* Spritz the cloth or floor duster with HC to clean and buff as you go. Shake area rugs outdoors. Wash if needed. Air-dry.

Monthly Eco-Freshness Thorough Breathe-able Cleaning = TC Gentle Reminders

- Look forward to the onset of each task with zing.
- Be mindful of your space.
  - Freshen the air:
  - open a window
  - spritz the air
  - diffuse an essential oil
- Tidy up: place all contents in their special storage area.
- Ceiling, light fixtures, ledges: spritz cloth or duster with HC to remove dust.
- Toilet and bowl: clean thoroughly with multiple tools.
  - close the toilet seat lid
  - Toilet tissue holder:
  - add a new roll to holder
  - fill stand
  - fold under ends to make a point
- Reading material: refresh and update.
- Drains: remove hair and buildup inside drains. Follow with my drain recipe.
- Sink: clean airflow hole, under rim, faucet base, and faucet.
- Mirror cabinet: wipe inside door, shelves, and products.
- Mirrors, glass, and windows: spritz and buff away smudges.
- Vanity: remove items, spritz, clean, buff; return items.
- Shower and bathtub: remove loose contents before cleaning.
- Bath and hand towels: wash, fold, return to proper area.
- Hamper: remove articles, wash, fold, return to proper area.
- Accessories: remove grimy buildup from personal care tools—brushes, sharpeners, sponges.
- Hamper: remove soiled articles, place in laundry room.
- Air-dry washcloths, bath gloves, and body brushes.
- Walls, switch plates, doors, knobs: spritz smudges, wipe.
- Wastebasket: empty, spritz, wipe. Replace eco-air freshener and specialty bag.

- Feed the plants: spritz with eco-air freshener.
- Floor and baseboards: clean, wipe, and buff as you go.
- Bath mats and area rugs:
    - shake outdoors
    - wash
    - air-dry
    - replace
- Release, Renew, Revitalize DIY eco-air fresheners.
- Unplug all plug-ables!
- Shopping list: add low-inventory items to the eco-inventory list.
- Spritz the air.
- Turn off lights.

Monthly Eco-Freshness
Thorough Breathe-able Cleaning = TC
Details

Accessories (personal care)	*Two tools: HC, Creamy Grit, cleaning & buffing cloths* Place personal care brushes, sharpeners, and sponges in the sink. Fill with tepid water and a splash of HC or shampoo. Wash and rinse each item until the water runs clean. Place on dry cloth to air-dry.
Shower/Bathtub	*Four tools: HC, Creamy Grit, scrubbing accessories, cleaning & buffing cloths* Remove loose items. Analyze the level of buildup. Use Creamy Grit and scrubbing accessories to remove spot discoloration in grout lines, tile, drains, and faucets, rinse. Spritz surfaces and loose items with HC—wipe, dry, buff. Wash shower curtain liner, air-dry, replace. Return items to proper storage.

Sink/Vanity Top	*Four tools: HC, Creamy Grit, scrubbing accessories, cleaning & buffing cloths* Remove products from vanity top. Clean surfaces with Creamy Grit and scrubbing accessories. Use a Q-tip and toothbrush for hard-to-reach areas—airflow hole, faucet base, sink rim. Spritz sink and vanity with HC, wipe, and buff. Wipe down "stuff" and return to proper area.
Toilet	*Five tools: HC, pumice stone or toilet brush, cleaning cloths, gloves, essential oil* Wear gloves to gently clean bowl with pumice stone to remove toilet bowl buildup and ring For a boosting clean and brightening, clean the inside and outside (base, too) with Creamy Grit and HC. When brushing, be certain to scrub up and under the rim. Wipe and buff all surfaces. Add two drops of an essential oil to the toilet bowl water. Do not flush.
Toilet Tissue Holder	*Three tools: HC, cleaning cloth, essential oil* Spritz cloth, wipe, and refill toilet tissue and essential oil air freshener.
Walls & Switch Plates + Doors & Knobs	*Three tools: HC, cleaning cloth, essential oil* Spritz cloth with HC to wipe away unwanted marks. Remove crayon and stickiness with lemon or lime essential oil.
Mirrors, Glass, Windows, + Light Fixture	*Two tools: Sparkle glass cleaner, cloth* Be gone, noticeable smudges. Spritz cloth, wipe, and buff.
Trash	*One pair of hands* Discard trash. Spritz HC over entire wastebasket, wipe, buff. Add a fresh scent eco-air freshener to the inside bottom of can. Add trash bag (optional).
Floor	*Two tools: HC, cloth* Remove all area rugs, mats, and accessories from the floor. Start at the furthest area and work toward the door to finish. Spritz the cleaning cloth with HC. Wipe, scrub, and buff as you go. Shake area rugs outdoors, wash, air-dry, and replace.

Spring + Fall Eco-Freshness
In-Depth Breathe-able Cleaning = IDBC
Gentle Reminders

Congratulations! No need to spend countless hours on spring and fall cleaning. You are ahead of the game by keeping up with weekly SC and monthly TC. IDBC tasks are minimized. Let's get to it and then go enjoy another beautiful day.

- Look forward to the onset of each task with zing.
- Be mindful of your space.
- Follow Monthly Eco-Freshness "Gentle Reminders," and "Details."

Spring and Fall Additions
- Light bulbs:
  - replace expired bulbs with LED
- Shower curtains:
  - remove
  - clean
  - air-dry
  - replace
- Window treatments:
  - remove
  - clean
  - replace
- Vents:
  - clean

Cabinets, Closets + Drawers
- This is the time to deep clean, change out liners, and DIY eco-air fresheners.
- Shopping list: add low-inventory items to the eco-inventory list.
- Spritz the air.
- Turn off lights.

JOY ••• 223

Spring + Fall
In-Depth Breathe-able Cleaning = IDBC
Details

Cabinets, Closets + Drawers	*Four tools: HC, scrubbing accessories, cleaning & buffing cloths* Remove contents and liners one section at a time. Spritz HC to thoroughly clean the inside and outside in its entirety—panels, edges, corners. Consolidate products and discard empties. Freshen up essentials and props with HC. Spritz or wash in the sink. Dry/air-dry thoroughly with cloths. Replace storage containers, drawer and shelf liners as needed. Freshen up or replace DIY eco-air fresheners, inside contents, and essential oil. Return items with organization.
Shower Curtains + Liners	*Tools: refer to cleaning instructions* Remove curtains and liners. Refer to cleaning instructions. Air-dry, press, and hang.
Vents	*Four tools: HC, scrubbing accessories, cleaning & buffing cloths* Spritz cloth with HC to remove all sorts of buildup. Use the small tools (toothbrush, Q-tip) to thoroughly clean corners. Spritz, wipe, buff.
Window Area	1. Remove window dressings 2. Remove screens 3. Clean glass and sill 4. Insert screens 5. Hang window dressings

Window Dressings	*Tools: refer to cleaning instructions* Remove window dressings. Refer to cleaning instructions. For a fresh look, replace and/or add trimmings to the current design. Reposition hardware to aesthetically create additional height and/or width.
Screens	*Four tools: Creamy Grit, HC, scrubbing brushes, cloths* Remove screens. Wash with Creamy Grit, HC, and a scrub brush in a laundry sink, bathtub, or outdoors. Rinse, air-dry, replace.
Windows	*Three tools: Sparkle glass cleaner, cleaning & buffing cloths* Remove storm windows. Clean glass and frame with glass cleaner. Buff and replace.
Trash	*One pair of hands* Discard trash. Spritz HC over entire wastebasket, wipe, buff. Add a fresh scent eco-air freshener to the inside bottom of can. Add trash bag (optional).
Sill	*Four tools: Creamy Grit, HC, scrubbing brushes, cloths* Clean sill and ledges with Creamy Grit and HC. Use small scrubbing tools (toothbrush, Q-Tip) to clean corners. Spritz once more. Dry and buff.

Intake a fresh breath of delicious, clean, breathe-able air.
Smile!
You did it!

Values Learned

- True beauty radiates from the inside out and the outside in.
- It's the little things that make a difference.
- To see.
- To remove the waste in the wastebasket daily.
- Never leave for later what should be done now.
- To think beyond the thought, be action-inspiring, and do it.
- To reach beyond my present state of comfort.
- Addressing the fine details is delightful.

Values learned

Now I Know

- 15 ml bottle of essential oils = ±300 drops!
- One cleaner: HC is for most surfaces.
- Protect the potency of essential oils with dark, colored glass bottles.
- Spray the cloth directly.
- Salt increases the cleaning power of baking soda.
- Vegetable glycerin maintains creaminess.
- Vodka and witch hazel extends the potency (longevity) of essential oil recipes.
- Switch out a recommended essential oil for a PP essential oil.
- Routinely clean with Charisse Marei's Breathe-able recipes to prevent toxic buildup.

Now I know

Adopting breathe-able clean methods preserves and enhances all life. Take this moment to acknowledge your accomplishments. Your conscious choice to free yourself and protect what you love most is revitalizing.

Share your Eco-Conscious approach to a beautiful Healthy Living Lifestyle with everyone to enhance their lives, too.

Your Story

Thoughts to Guide Your Thinking

- I am most grateful for . . .
- A clear mind is a healthy mind . . .
- A squeaky clean journey . . .

What is my gift for clean?

Breathe-able you.
On to Chapter 7!

7

Eco-Conscious Design

PASSION .....

To transform a blank canvas
or a single object
into a living breathing picture is an injection of euphoria.

My Story
A Special Place

Which bathroom composition do I share with you? Over the years, I designed and redesigned quite a few. What Eco-Conscious interior design project propels me with a zest to guide you through a rewarding process of empowerment for your project? What thoughts made my heart beat faster?

All along this book journey, I shared personal stories stemming from my childhood home, specifically my first bathroom. I felt it only natural to continue the process though advancing in time. Interior design inspirations of my present home fulfill the quest of an Eco-Conscious approach to a beautiful Healthy Living Lifestyle. After all, if I am not living, breathing, and eating green, how can I imagine you to do the same?

Welcome to my home—though be prepared, for once you cross over the threshold, the exterior world softly melts away, as do the to-do lists and emotional woes of life. Simplicity and joyful happenings are at the helm. You will discover that a passion for radiant energy and continuity is methodical, subtly echoing through intentional elements to engage the senses, rhythm, balance, use of color, crystals, and materials. Once my story concludes, you may feel encouraged to linger a bit longer.

The aspiration of each bathroom and half bath is to reflect the same unifying elements. Each expresses my personal style story of a holistic environment inspired by nature, supporting inner and outer beauty and well-being. As you step into each sanctuary, your senses fully awaken as your spirit is lifted. You begin to feel one within the space, to experience the warmth, the light, clean airiness, balance, and the harmonious flow of timeless elegance. Eco-Conscious green design is present along with an intentional spiritual element, unifying each of these rooms together.

The European elegance of the main house flows seamlessly into each special little haven. Every bathroom and half bath is embellished with a common thread—a unifying element felt intuitively, for once the door closes, the space is between "it" and "you." The question to ask: Will you embrace the space feeling a unity, a connection, a level of comfort? After all, the main reason to enter, to be part of the bathroom, is to Release, Renew, Revitalize.

I understood the purpose, style, and the user of each of these personal and semi-private rooms. Making reference to drawings and material specifications as well as paying attention to selections of the main house throughout the design process were paramount. Removing the potential for mishaps simplified the design process. New selections were introduced as well as organizational pieces, recycled art work, mirrors, and favored window dressings from years gone by. The warmth of the neutral light and airy color palette included creamy lights, soft blue hues, and peaceful greens. Dilution of the same hues flowed gracefully through the main circulation, entertaining areas, private rooms, and into other special little havens.

Whether redesigning, updating, or refreshing the room, each process of simultaneously selecting essentials remained the same. The difference lay within the functionality and aesthetics of each individual sanctuary. I will take you on a journey through the process of designing one of the smaller special havens to "K.I.S.S."

Use my eco-interior design story as a guide for your project, no matter how big or small.

Eco-Design with Passion

My passion for small spaces is exceptional, and the half bath is no exception. The half baths are the smallest rooms in my home. One in particular is located on the main floor midway between the front and rear of the house. Visuals are seen into this tiny space from various viewpoints such as the music room, kitchen, and the transition to and from the main hall.

What does the eye see while glancing toward the half bath? What image is captured? Is it the natural light that filters through the window dressing, or is it the subtle glow from the single candlestick? Did one notice the tiny framed artwork positioned just below the window frame that reads:

> "Love
> transcends all time.
> It is a voice inside the heart
> that never stops
> singing."
> —Unknown

There is so much more than what meets the eye of a passerby. It's the thought process, the passion, and the energetic connection that one feels, which is portrayed in the overall composition. There is no main focal point. Each individual vignette is a picture within itself. A subtle ahh is mindlessly released.

The foundation of the half bath, which measures six-by-six-by-nine feet, began with two of my most favored tiles left over from the gathering room floor and kitchen backsplash. In one hand, I held an aged creamy-hued limestone tile infused with meandering gray veining. In the other hand was the most intriguing handmade European white-and-soft-green tile adorned with an inlay of miniature cut crystal glass.

I thought, How can I discard the extras into a rubbish pile? Their intrinsic nature has so much substance. Of all the hundreds of tiles I had seen, none compared to the organic beauty of what was before me. I gathered every last tile and designed the floor. One-inch square glass tiles were inset into a two-by-two-foot central area to form a diamond. Individual limestone tiles of various geometric sizes were placed around the inset to form a random pattern. As I stood looking at my masterpiece, my eyes widened as I did the happy dance. A work of art was created. Each adjoining tile, from the first to the last, was as breathtakingly important as the next to complete the composition.

Gorgeously gratifying

Oh, those walls! These darling havens were destined to have their own unifying element separate from the main house. Transforming blank canvas walls into a colorful splendor to capture the soul and imagination was key. My goal was to reach beyond a splash of color from a can. I envisioned a luxurious print extending from floor to ceiling enhancing the verticality and natural splendor of the space. To my absolute delight I found myself captivated by an ecology line of wallpaper. Endless works of art dripped off the page. Each wall covering signified a work of art, a reflection of my unique eco-design style story of natural elements, timeless elegance, favored soft hues, and delightful whimsical patterns. The swirl motif chosen for this powder room expressed no boundaries as it subtly changed form, conforming to one's imagination.

I am . . . forever fascinated

My desire was to mimic this approach in the tall single window dressing design. With pencil and paper in hand, I sketched my favored balloon-style designs above cafe curtains. The design concept was spot-on to enrich the natural grandeur of nature and to create privacy.

I set an appointment with my go-to workroom to fabricate the window dressing. For the balloon shade I chose a shimmering green silk textile with a repeated diamond/ogee pattern. It harmonized with the swirl paper in pattern, texture, and color. To bring a bit of dazzle into the design, the gentle curve of the balloon shade was trimmed in dangling light-blue and green crystals. Hanging a mere six inches below on an inside-mounted gold matte-iron rod were fourteen coordinating rings to support a pair of delicate, white shear pinch-pleat curtains. Whether glancing out the window or tinkling while on the toilet, you gently embrace a picturesque view of nature while nature quietly takes hold of you.

Natural elements continue to flow through the tranquility of the concealed vanity, expressing clean lines and simple form. Atop the wooden base rests the carving of a thirty-six-inch honed travertine stone vanity top with an integrated rectangular bowl. The backsplash features five hand-cut limestone tiles in a stepping fashion ready to absorb mindless little splashes. Pairing exceptionally well with the sink composition's elegance is a finely sculpted, bridge-style faucet with individual cross knobs and Euro-influenced white porcelain hot and cold inlays. For a spa-like touch, 284 half-inch two-tone, smooth glass stones bejewel the sink basin for therapeutic and playful purposes, especially for the young at heart.

Centered above the sink hangs an aged European-inspired antique gold mirror flanked by two elegant sconces finished in luminescent gold dust and dazzling crystal jewels. While looking into the mirror, it's only natural to see the reflection of a favored two-by-four-foot French poster whimsically portraying a burst of playful pastel flowers. I recall the day, some twenty-six years ago, when Mother and I purchased this print, titled Encore de Fleurs, from a local shop. I knew then, as I know now, this print would travel a lifetime with me and within me.

I reflect—I smile

The Persuade toilet by Kohler, positioned next to the sink, has dual-flush technology designed to conserve water. Minimal intentional appointments pull the design together. A repurposed Michael Aram lemonwood candle lid rests over the dual-flush button. Defining the space above the toilet is a shapely wooden shelf finished in aged silver, gold, and black tones. The simplicity of its scale and function prevents a clutter feeling. Sitting within arms' reach is a round, fluted glass aromatic spray bottle in a splash of color. A press of the finger atop the pump releases an array of molecules to instantly transform the breathe-able air into heavenly delight.

A healthy greenery in a small refurbished white terra-cotta clay pot sits atop an ornate stone garden stool to enhance breathe-able air and natural beauty. To prevent moisture between the materials, the planter sits securely on three stoneware pot feet—though it's easy to understand why one might question the law of gravity, for it appears as if there are just two feet, presenting the illusion of the pot partially suspended in floating air. A bit of mystique also encompasses the stool. Depending on the time of day, one may be fortunate to see a subtle illumination gently glowing through the free-form spaces.

Positioned against the wall between the toilet and vanity composition is a rustic white iron tissue caddy beautified with delicate, decorative, frosted glass-like leaves. Both materials form the space to store three backup rolls of tissue paper and one usable roll. The ceramic wastebasket is conveniently positioned on the left-hand side of the vanity. Concealed storage is purposeful. Open the vanity doors to reveal two stacked rows of white, unscented bamboo toilet tissue, sugarcane and bamboo tissue boxes, and treeless napkins. The two drawers house artfully designed white linen hand towels, feminine products, organic cotton wool buds, hair accessories, and Thieves therapeutic hand soap, dental floss, and wipes.

    I chose to share this powder room with you because I love the space. Yes, it is small, but it is what you do with a space—any space—that matters.

I am sitting in the kitchen at the island in deep thought while writing a story to you. As I sit back, slightly tilting my head to the left, my eyes rest on the window in the half bath. I see the sparkling light filtering through the open white sheer fabric, and branches of the birch tree swaying gently. Energetically, it feels good. I smile.

    I see it, I use it, every day, and several times throughout the day. It is widely utilized by family members, friends, and guests to linger, to embrace the natural splendor. It is the second-smallest room in the house. The other is the half bath on the lower level that I also designed for a purpose and with purpose.

Before You Begin

To eliminate a clutter feeling, our focus is on One Room at a Time and not the entire house. We know the big picture is for your special haven to reflect an inviting Eco-Conscious, Healthy-Living Lifestyle. Zone in. The key is to tap into your senses. Listen to that internal stirring of an inspirational idea and an unexpected OMG prompt from a must-have work of art, tile, fixture, color, and so on.

These are your foundational tools to build upon. Once you identify your inspiring idea, write it down. Transition from there to define your purpose. Visualize the transformation and the resplendent energy felt upon completion. Read my story once more for guidance.

The bathroom is a unifying space.
To cleanse.
To nourish.
To transform
into a beautiful, enlightened being.

Consciously strive toward your goal one step at a time. Set up a system to organize ideas, notes, material samples, and tools. Enjoy trying my Eco-Conscious PPs. Use as a reference to guide you along a rewarding path to unveil your unique personal style story and authentic flair. Unlike the chapters before, we will continuously add tools to the interior design toolbox.

As with all things in life, it begins with the planting of a seed.

seed

Tools of the Trade

Eco-Consciousness is a necessity, not a luxury, as you gather Tools of the Trade to manifest the bathroom and half bath eco-design. Enhance performance with drawings, samples, materials, product selections, how-to's, and tips.

Create a material specification sheet for each bathroom and half bath. Include date, contact, store/vendor, description name, quantity, material, pattern, color, style number, cost, date received. Update the spec sheet with new additions. Remove outdated information.

Drawings

Stepping it up a notch! Regardless of the scope of your project, visuals are a useful guide for clarity, continuity, and inspiration. Produce pieces of creative work through a One Room at a Time design board, sketches, a scale floor plan, and elevations.

The level of detail and type of drawings are influenced by your drawing ability and intricacy of the project. Opt for the feel of the traditional hands-on approach or be consciously green with online design and photo-editing software. It's a PP. Either way the journey will, as I always say, "Transform your vision into reality."

One Room at a Time Design Board

A One Room at a Time design board, otherwise known as a color, sample, mood, or inspiration board, is inspiring, purposeful, and artful. Create one for each bathroom and half bath.

To clarify your personal style, gather sketches and images from various sources—books, magazines, social media, showroom displays. Visit sample model bathrooms or friends' homes for inspiration. Place the images directly on the design board. Recognize common themes. As the project develops, you will sense which visuals to keep and which to discard.

Create A Board—Hands On
- Take photos and gather samples of essentials that remain in the space.
- Collect samples—paint, wallpaper, fabric, wood, tile, stone, glass, finishes . . .
- Gather images—full bathroom, mini compositions, storage, small props, accessories, fixtures, wall and window designs, towels . . .

- Cut samples into smaller pieces with a pair of sharp scissors.
- Arrange samples on the board to determine the board size.
- Draw a pencil line. Place the ruler on top of the line and cut with an X-acto knife.
- Adhere samples with a mini pin, paper clip, and adhesive.

Sketch It Up

Sketches are optional though useful to provide insight into a variety of ways to utilize the space. Transfer ideas to paper. With pencil and paper or electronic device, draw a sketch or two of the floor plan. Sketch elevation drawings of the entire room or a vignette of one section. No need for perfection. This step provides a visual sense of clarity. When ready, proceed to the next step.

PP: 2H lead pencil

Eco-Tip . . . H lead presents crisp clean lines.

Charisse Marei's Measuring Basics

1. Stand at the entry door looking into the bathroom. Select a starting point. Lightly sketch the outline of the floor. Begin with perimeter walls, interior walls, closets, then continue with bump-outs.

2. Sketch in doors and windows with a line on the plan to indicate placement. Openings do not include trim.

3. Sketch in essentials to remain—builtins, freestanding furniture, toilet, vanity . . .

4. Take measurements.

5. Add measurements to the sketch and measurement sheet.

6. Add photos.

Tools for thought:
foam board, images, paint samples
paper, pencil, poster board
ruler, X-acto knife, spec sheet

Gather tools

Sketch it up

To Scale

Transfer the floor plan sketch into a scale drawing. Since the focus is on one room, the recommended scale is 1/2 inch = 1 foot. Once the plan is complete, use it as a reference to guide you through the decision process for present and future enhancements. The next time you find that perfect "something," make sure it fits before purchasing. It's the equivalent of purchasing a new pair of shoes.

It's
the look,
the feel,
the fit,
The purchase!
The enjoyment!

Floor Plans + Elevations—By Hand

To draw a basic scale floor plan and elevations by hand is a simple quick learn. Several drawing tools are required for the process to flow with ease. My go-to designer tools include a back-lit drafting table, light board, magnetic room planner, graph paper, pencil, eraser, stickies, and hard-edge ruler. DIY: make freestanding templates to scale. Move around on the plan to a desired spot.

PP: Magnetic Space Planning System, The Board Residential Room Planner

Tip . . . Graph paper simplifies the process with accuracy.

Create Scale Drawings—Hands On

Gather	sketches and measurements.
Secure	the four corners of the drawing paper to a fixed surface.
Draw	a hard line scale floor plan using designer tools from your toolbox.
Redraw	measurements to scale, 1/2 inch = 1 foot.

Floor Plan

- Draw perimeter walls.
- Draw interior walls.
- Erase door opening lines. Add windows, fixtures . . .
- Elevations
- Draw items of importance, one wall at a time.
- Add each essential.

DIY Versatile Templates
draw to scale
cut out shape
place on plan

Floor Plans + Elevations—Design Software

Perhaps you are searching for a user-friendly online interior design tool to satisfy your techie persona and space-planning needs. Software options are vast and created for the novice to the professional. Discover real-world materials and finishes to sense the room in its entirety before spending a penny to remove a wall or a single tile. Look for simple options, for instance, the ability to change the two-dimension plan into a 3-D view. This option is one of many. Choose mindfully.

PP: 3Dream 3D Design

Eco-Tip . . . Electronic Device. The larger the monitor screen, the easier the process.

Keep drawings and measurements together.

Transfer drawings

246 ··· *Eco-Conscious Design*

Eco-Style Story

Unveil the one thought inspiring your palette. Is it . . .
- relaxing in the warmth of a freestanding tub while engrossed in a romantic suspense novel?
- gazing into a favored work of art?
- a new wall application revealing dimension, color, and architectural detail?
- a dazzling crystal chandelier dangling from an inspiring ceiling treatment?

When you find that one "thing" that inspires you (you may already own it), begin to design the space around it. As your style story develops, the overall feel of the room is set in motion.

Gather the file images and samples acquired. Spread them on a table, or position yourself in the bathroom or half bath. Identify the common thread expressed in style, material, pattern, texture, and color. A solid foundation is present.

Select the greenest materials to nurture your whole being from the inside out and the outside in. My PPs were discovered through years of a passionate, purposeful process. Ultimately, it is your PP to complement your style story that will take precedence in your bathroom and not the current fashion trend. Trust your inner self. When you feel a burst of positive energy from within, go with it!

My eco-Style Story

Eco Style

Let's continue to unveil just a few of my favorite "eco" things that perhaps you have yet to discover . . .

Walls
Windows
Greenery

Primary + Secondary Essentials

Must-haves are the primary essentials, the staple pieces—sink, shower, bathtub, toilet, faucets, and tub fillers that provide functionality to these special havens. Secondary essentials are the treasures we've come to rely on in our daily fare such as mirrors, tile, fluff, aromatics, and window dressings. As a whole the essentials enhance the quality of personal needs to satisfy a desire, release negative energy, renew the senses, and revitalize well-being.

Refer to the 3Rs before purchasing new essentials.

Release . . .	Remove unrepairable and inefficient essentials. Replace with eco-friendly, efficiently repurposed, reconditioned, or new.
Renew . . .	Repair and replace to restore functionality and aesthetics with eco-friendly, efficiency, and conservation at the forefront.
Revitalize . . .	Bring new eco-friendly, efficient, conservation essentials into the space.

Natural Beau Walls

Have you thought about the role of your bathroom walls? Those strong, beautiful vertical walls support a rhythmic flow in your physical being, consciousness, and subliminal mind. Your eyes may rest on the vertical surface for a nanosecond, engage in mindless snapshots, or settle with an oblivious stare. Walls stand tall to support, protect, and nourish your well-being. What is your role to support those walls? To lavish them with delicious eco-nourishment from the inside to the outer surface adornment, of course.

You may think, My theme is in place as are my walls. Now what? Do I open a can of paint, unroll a sheet of wallpaper, adhere tile, affix architectural detail, or all of the above?

Explore the options. For instance, choosing a wall adornment in the perfect hue is the energetic icing on the gluten-free cake! It's where we begin.

*When you consciously find that "perfect color,"
the cycle of inspiration and harmonious balance unfolds.
It captivates its audience.
Projects the mood.
Awakens the senses.
Dances with light.
Plays with geometry.*

The hue of choice is a reflection of inner inspiration stemming from your unique personality.

To find your color of influence, begin with the process of elimination. Open the paint fan deck or individual color cards. Quickly remove colors from the palette that prompt a questionable thought, zapping a joyful approach. Hop, skip, run, or walk to your sanctuary. Hold the remaining color samples up one at a time. Close one eye and keep the other eye wide open. Slowly turn your body, envision the color on the wall. The perfect color satisfies a blissful state of knowing, setting the mode envisioned. Is it bright and cheery, earthy and serene, stimulating, warm, or cozy? Does the hue satisfy your senses and well-being in its totality?

Continue with the selection of eco-friendly wall finishes such as paint, clay, wallpaper, wood, and tile to work synergistically, unifying the overall theme. Add a twist of feng shui by adding drops of pure essential oil into the paint. The key is to listen to your inner self. I found, time and time again, this approach manifests heartfelt beautification, supporting the alignment between one's spiritual self and the space.

BREATHE-ABLE PAINT WITH A TWIST OF FENG SHUI

Add an essential oil to counteract VOCs[3], set-forth aromatic walls, and to shift the energy of the room.

Gather	Blend	Manifest
paint	essential oil (PP)	colorful emotion
	50 drops per one gallon of paint	
	15 ml bottle per five gallons of paint	
	add*stir*sniff	

DROPS

LET'S DO IT
Intention the essential oil of choice is in alignment with the intention to manifest for the space.
Choose an essential oil.
Identify your intention. With each drop of essential oil and stir of the stick, express your intention.
add*stir*go

Eco-Conscious Wall Considerations

Buy local . . . support local businesses while minimizing your consumer footprint.
Recycle materials . . . donate to an organization in your local community.
Storage safety . . . keep in original container. Seal the lid. Store in a detached storage area.

---

3 **VOCs** are solvents that are released into the air as paint dries. They can cause acute symptoms, including headaches and dizziness.

Eco-Conscious Paint + Finishes

Look for environmentally responsible, sustainable brands. Refer to the label before purchasing—paint, primer, stains, varnishes, wood finishes, sealers, adhesive, caulk, and added colored pigments. Look for little to no toxicity, natural mineral pigments, water-based, zero VOC, and no odor.

PP: AFM Safecoat and Miss Mustard Seeds Milk Paint

Eco-Tip . . . Add drops of a single or blend pure essential oil to each can. Label the can.

Eco-Conscious Clay Paints

The air remains breathe-able as do the walls with the application of eco clay paints. The ingredients are 100 percent natural clay and natural mineral pigments, and yes this includes the luscious colors. The product absorbs odors and is mold resistant, and fire resistant.

PP: American Clay offers unique textures to enhance tranquility.

Eco-Tip . . . Elevate the potency with Charisse Marei's breathe-able paint recipe.

Eco-Conscious Powdered Milk Paint (and more)

The product line fits nicely into the environmentally responsible category. Ingredients are of natural & non-toxic synthetic pigments. You will love the texture (powder), packaging (pretty bag), and gorgeous colors. Additional products of interest—hemp oil, beeswax finish, wax puck, antiquing and furniture wax, and brush soap to clean tools of the trade.

PP: Miss Mustard Seeds Milk Paint

Eco-Tip . . . Always prep the surface.

Eco-Conscious Wallpaper

The "pick me" wallpaper blends beauty with eco-chic compositions. Look for naturally woven fibers such as bamboo, reed, seagrass (grasscloth), and water-based paints, inks, and dyes. Before making selections read the labels—paper, coatings, backings, and paste. Walk away from vinyl, VOCs, heavy metals found in dyes and inks, and fireproofing (except for borate, a natural mineral).

PP: Patty Madden Ecology—Harmony

Eco-Tip . . . For continuity choose one wallpaper designer for bathrooms and half baths.

Eco-Conscious Tile Coverings (floors, too)

Floors are a focal point of beauty. An array of eco-savvy, innovative, sustainable products are increasing in popularity and popping up in the tile industry. Consider stone, concrete, cork, ceramic, porcelain, glass, metal, and bamboo. Look for materials with minimal impact on our Earth that are locally sourced, renewable, and have high recycled content as well as natural ecological and natural plant-based pigments. You may discover the look and feel of porcelain tile is the optimum solution to transform the space without the use of real natural materials. It's a PP. Do note that product certification is on the rise.

    PP: Jeffrey Court—inset deco tiles with inlay crystals.

    Eco-Tip . . . Lay tile close together to minimize grout lines.

Eco-Conscious Grout

Finish the project with innovative, eco-friendly grout. Replace the standard chemical-laden grout with a grout that is non-toxic, requires no water to mix and no sealing, and is resistant to mold, mildew, and stains.

    PP: Nontoxic QuartzLock2 urethane grout

    Eco-Tip . . . Choose a color closest to the main color of the floor and wall material.

Details please

Dressing Your Windows

Close your eyes. Reminisce about a time while in the presence of a naked window—no dressing or architectural details. The window appeared as undressed geometry, and as a consequence the shape became the focal point. How did you feel in the room? Uncomfortable? Exposed? Now, imagine reentering the room. The window, dressed in lustrous textures of natural fibers and fine detail, no longer expresses drawn lines of geometry but is an expression of life, presenting a harmonious, rhythmic flow engaging your senses.

Dare to be creatively surprising with designs that are irresistibly inviting. You see, window fashions elevate the overall composition, feel, and function of a room, and are an expression of your personal style story. The design dictates fabric selection, accessories, hardware placement, lighting, privacy, and unity. With all the trimmings in place they are often the main focal point and dictate the mood regardless of style, material, quantity, size, or location.

In the open position, window fashions create a frame interweaving splendid views of the natural and built environment effortlessly within the room. While closed, the dressing in all its natural beauty embraces the walls like a masterpiece. Windows with integrated architectural detail, mullions, stained glass, a special shape, or a unique location are themselves a statement within themselves and may require no additional adornments.

Gather design ideas from window books. Sketch drawings. To visually expand the room dimensions, use one of my camouflaging tools. To add height, position hardware outside the window frame and closer to the ceiling and extend the side panels to touch or drape onto the floor. To lengthen the wall, mount the hardware beyond window frame standards and add additional fabric to create a sense of fullness. The key is to balance the treatments to the right- and left-hand sides of the window and, of course, within the room. Add sketches to the design board. Enjoy the process.

Sketch up drawings

Personal Window Dressing Remake

I envisioned a timeless light, airy, elegant window fashion to complement the new master bathroom theme. I opened a dresser drawer to reveal two custom single panels neatly tucked inside. In my former home, they gracefully hung in the dressing area on two single windows. As I stretched out the panels before me, I marveled at the simplicity and beauty of the ecru tone-on-tone, lace panels embellished in a floral-leaf pattern and trimmed in clear dangling crystals. Undoubtedly, the time arrived for these favored panels to come out and undergo a remake.

The transformation embraces a double window fashion exemplifying my vision. Those darling crystals adorn a light and airy ballon-style shade. An outside board-mount replaces the former rod and is fastened nine inches below the ceiling line. A single loop cord positioned to the left-hand side permits raising and lowering the shade to various intervals. It's a PP as to when to raise and gather for the most fluff and natural exposure and when to lower to full expansion for privacy.

Eco-Conscious Window Considerations

Select eco-green products to support fresh, therapeutic, breathe-able air in your home. Look for eco-friendly, biodegradable, green, recycled materials, renewable (sustainable) fabrics, and certified organic materials, including but not limited to cotton, silk, wool, linen, hemp, reeds, bamboo, jute, and hardwoods.

Invest in energy efficient windows and a window film to provide insulation, reflect heat, reduce glare and noise, and extend the longevity of those fashionable window dressings.

Reduce environmental impact. Choose quality, durability, and longevity over quantity. Buy local, recycle, remake, or donate. Repurpose or redesign window fashions to suit your personal style story and window. When a panel is too short, add a coordinating fabric to extend length. Add a trim.

PP: Charisse Marei's window designs

Eco-Tip . . . Coordinate two window fashion designs within one room.

Eco-Reference Guide—Window Considerations

Refer to the mini eco-key word reference guide to Release, Renew, Revitalize window dressings. Add new favorites to the list. Your pathway to beautiful Eco-Conscious window fashions is well on its way.

Happy Designing + Eco-Shopping!

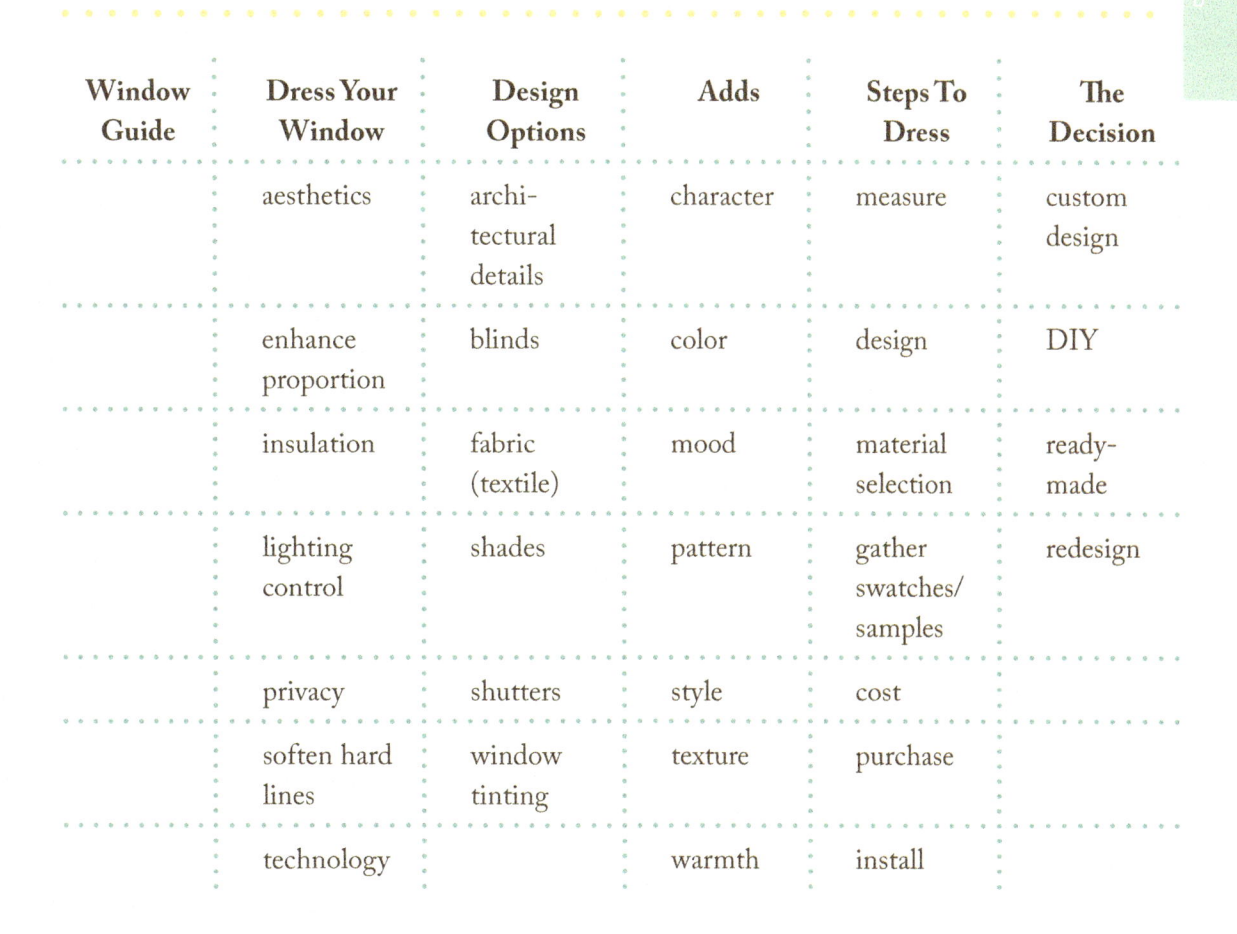

Window Guide	Dress Your Window	Design Options	Adds	Steps To Dress	The Decision
	aesthetics	architectural details	character	measure	custom design
	enhance proportion	blinds	color	design	DIY
	insulation	fabric (textile)	mood	material selection	ready-made
	lighting control	shades	pattern	gather swatches/samples	redesign
	privacy	shutters	style	cost	
	soften hard lines	window tinting	texture	purchase	
	technology		warmth	install	

PASSION • • • 257

Measure Guide

- One worksheet = One window
- Use a steel measuring tape for accuracy.
- Write down each measurement.
- Take measurements twice for accuracy.
- Measure the distance between multiple windows on the same wall.
- Record final measurements to the nearest one-eighth-inch.
- _____
- _____
- _____

Inside Mounted

- Window treatments hang inside the window frame.
- Take three horizontal and vertical measurements. Start from left to right and top to bottom.
  - top
  - middle
  - bottom
  - left
  - center
  - right
- Record the narrowest measurements.

- Measure the window recess. The design must allow for the rod, mounting board, or shutters.

-

-

-

Outside Mounted

- Window treatments hang outside the window frame.

- Increase fullness with additional fabric.

- To exaggerate the window height and room dimensions, hang the treatments several inches lower than the ceiling or crown moulding.

- To exaggerate the window width and room dimensions, hang the treatments beyond the industry standards.

- Combine the two approaches to increase overall height and width.

-

-

-

Hardware Guide

- Rod with rings. Measure from the bottom of rings to the desired length.
- Rod pocket treatments. Note the pocket opening size. Note the diameter of the rod. Measure from the top of rod to the desired length.
- Look for hardware finished with low to no VOC paint.
-
-
-

Eco-Tips

- Print worksheet copies as needed.
- Protect the longevity of drapery fabric with a backing.
- Choose one backing fabric and color to enhance exterior aesthetics.
- Increase fullness with additional fabric.
- Be consistent when taking and recording measurements.

Live, Air-Cleansing Greenery

Bring a touch of healthy living nature into your sanctuary. Add fresh greenery and splashes of lush flowery color to beautify and enhance indoor air quality (IAQ).

Live healthy plants purify the air. They absorb particulates while simultaneously consuming carbon dioxide and releasing oxygen, filling the room with breathe-able clean air. I was elated to learn of a study conducted by NASA scientists revealing certain houseplants absorb, hence remove, approximately 85 percent of indoor air pollutants while purifying the air. Do note that once you add a single plant, the energy of the space instantly transforms, too.

First, discover your plant style. Next up: Define your eco-style design through one or multiple compositions. Will you suspend plants in midair, a wall display, or on a stand, shelf, sill, or bathtub surround? Take action-inspiring steps to display life.

Arrangements

- Air plants in salt holders, shells, glass planters, or copper vessels
- Decorative or terra-cotta clay pots
- Hanging plants in clay pots
- Hanging string gardens
- Live wall: framed art or free-form
- Live mini wreath
- Tiered reclaimed-wood wall planter
- Wall garden
- Wall pockets in airy mesh pouches

Each day I take notice to the three slender clear glass cylinders perched on the bathroom window sill. All three contain a mini green air plant rooted in semiprecious stones.

Symbolically, positive chi radiates from the plants as delight embraces my being. Memories of my granddaughter Natalie surface as I recall her tiny hands removing one plant at a time and placing on the bathtub surround. Together we stooped on the floor to enjoy the fantastical gift from nature. As we laughed out loud, she did the happy dance. We lightly spritzed the leaves with the Burst of Sunshine Air Freshener, then back to the sill they went.

Cleansing Plants

Plant + Botanical Name	Air-borne Toxins Removed	Code B=benzine CM = carbon monoxide F = formaldehyde M = mold T = trichloroethylene X = xylene
Aloe	Aloe Barbadensis	B, C, M, F
Bamboo palm	Chamaedorea Seifrizii	B, F, T
Boston fern	Nephrolepis exaltata 'Bostoniensis'	F, X
Chinese evergreen	Aglaonema Modestrum	VARIETY
English Ivy	Hedera helix	B, F, M
Chrysanthemum/ floral mum	Chrysanthemum morifolium	B, F
Gerbera daisy	Gerbera jamesonii	B, T
Golden pothos	Epipremnum aureum	A, B, F, X
Moth orchid	Phalaenopsis	F, VOCs
Peace lily	Spathiphyllum	B, F, T, X
Snake plant	Sansevieria trifasciata	B, F, T
Weeping fig	Ficus benjamina	B, F, T

List the primary essential must-haves to satisfy your eco-style and to compliment your healthy living sanctuary.

Happy, Healthy Eco-Shopping!

Values Learned

- All things begin with the planting of a seed, the flourishing of a thought.
- Beauty begins from within and expresses itself boundlessly.
- To live, breathe, and eat green is contagious.
- Simplicity and joyful happenings are at the helm of the heart, the home.
- To tap into my senses, listening to that internal stirring of inspiration.
- To consciously allow the cycle of inspiration and harmonious balance to unfold.

Values learned

Now I Know

- A holistic environment is inspired by nature supporting all forms of beauty.
- What the eye sees is the image of the energy captured by the soul.
- Research until I find that special "thing."
- To focus on one room at a time brings forth clarity, confidence.
- Always remove outdated stuff.
- Close both eyes and visualize to see what is yet to be in the physical space.

Now I know

Your Story

Thoughts to Guide Your Thinking

- Reveal an interior design story that makes your heart beats faster ...
- Describe your thought process, passion, and energetic connection ...
- A unifying element ...

What bathroom design or redesign project comes forth with ease?

Your journey continues.
On to Chapter 8!

8

Water Consciousness

AWARENESS

The act of improving the water
within our bodies
is at the same time
the act of improving the water
that covers our planet.
...
So once you love and appreciate the water inside yourself,
you can improve the water of the world.

—Masaru Emoto

My Story

Thinking Beyond the Toothbrush

As I cupped the icy-cold, crystal-clear water in my hands, I noticed its purity. Then ten quick splashes of refreshing bursts of . . . ahh! Up and over my face to rejuvenate and stay youthful. There was no smell. Nor did I use more than needed. And so my story begins.

I was oblivious to what is now so clear. For three fashionably steamy-hot months, a subliminal message was delivered daily—under my nose and across my taste buds, though I could not see it, hear it, or feel it. The message was, so to speak, the planting of a seedling, part of my future yet to be discovered.

The year was 1973. When cousins Pamela and Jillian extended an informal invitation to spend the summer months on their father's farm, I accepted with enthusiasm. I vaguely recall our traveling from the East Coast to the Midwest city of Concord, Ohio. Upon arrival, and to my surprise, our transportation from the airport was in a quirky, old-fashioned pickup truck. That is when I met Uncle Don, a brawny and compelling man, and all six of his children. As we traveled to his farm, I embraced nature in its purest form. The lushness of endless organic greenery rising and stretching boundless underneath the heavenly sky and the oh-so-delicious dewy, sweet scent blowing through the atmosphere remains as a majestic imprint in my mind.

We passed countless acres of family-owned farms before approaching what was to be called home for the following months. Perched around the bend of a long driveway sat a weathered yet welcoming old white wooded farmhouse, detached barn, and silo. On the other side of the road, across from the dwellings, glorious views of infinite sky connected with an endless open field where only green grass grew. Little did I know, our morning ritual would be a gallop to that very field before opening to full expansive runs.

Paradise on Earth!

Adapting to the farming lifestyle came with ease. Once a week, we extended our early morning horse ride, trotting into a nearby town. Being a conscious fashionista, my confidence was bubbling as I hopped on my horse wearing a favored pair of worn hipster blue jeans, wide brown leather belt, bandanna top, and girly cowboy boots. Folded into tiny squares and tucked deep inside a sock were two dollar bills and bits of change. Upon arrival, we strapped the worn leather reins to the wooden post outside the town store. I took notice of my surroundings. Every limb of my body and beat of my heart connected with the earthy scenery of dirt roads and minimalistic wooden buildings. Onward we went to buy our private stash of sweets.

Our daily journeys were hot and long as we traveled to the distant upper fields to pick corn. Uncle Don sat at the helm of the tractor while all thirteen of us youngsters bounced on the attached wooden flatbed. The incline steadily increased along the narrow dirt road while steep, unsettling drop-offs hovered to our left. Once on flat ground, I danced with glee. As we hand-picked corn, my whole being felt the mass of solar energy. The sizzling rays meandered between the thick, tall stalks to find little me. A drop of drinkable water was not to be had.

By horse or on foot, we were mindful of the sun's position, making certain to return to the farm as the last beam of daylight stretched across the night sky. Sounds of unfamiliar wildlife prompted a sense of unknowing, edging me closer to my horse as an ominous feeling encapsulated my being. Thoughts of a panther pouncing on us lurked in my mind. It wasn't until the horses were secure in the stable and we turned the round knob to the front door that I felt safe once again.

The family room, bathroom, and our transformed bedroom are the only rooms I recall. At each day's end, everyone gathered in the family room around Uncle Don as he sat in his oversized recliner. The youngsters sat on the floor and on the old distressed sofa, laughing while sharing stories, followed by a trip to the bathroom before turning in for the night.

A functional outhouse was present on the property, though that is all I know. My recollection of the in-house bathroom located at the top of four stairs remains vague. I do remember conserving water was at the forefront, resulting in a quick in-and-out and no special "me time." The room was small with a shortage of embellishments. In its simplest form, it offered basic essentials, a white toilet, bathtub, and a single bowl sink. However, my eyes moved around the muted yellow stains. Never before had I utilized a dirty, dysfunctional bathroom. The toilet never flushed properly and the bathtub sported a permanent ring. After squeezing the minty toothpaste along my new toothbrush bristles, I turned the sink water on. To my surprise, the water was exceptionally clear and glacial cold. But that smell! What was that odor lurking beyond my toothbrush?

The smell transported my thoughts to home. I envisioned myself standing at the freestanding brown gas stove, staring intensely at the pot of boiling eggs as they rhythmically bounced to the music playing inside my head. My mother's voice overrode my thoughts as I squeezed my nostrils ever so tightly and ran to the window gasping for a breath of fresh air.

"Oh, Mom! What was that smell?"

"A rotten egg," she replied.

The offensive odor emitting from the faucet was that of rotten eggs. Decades later, the subliminal message I'd received at the age of twelve came forth to my conscious awareness, for I learned the water contained hydrogen sulfide. According to the Water Research Center, hydrogen sulfide (gas) is often found in household water—coming from the hot water heater, water softener, or the well. It is written that low concentrations do not pose serious health effects. Today, I test my water.

Oh my!
At the age of twelve I was of unconscious mind . . .
Drinkable water varied in content.
Drinkable water affects well-being.
Sustainable consumerism was such a "thing?"
Nor did I imagine global water vulnerability.

Before You Begin

H_2O
colorless * odorless * tasteless * transparent
Water is precious.
A valuable natural resource.
Pure water
Releases impurities.
Renews our body.
Revitalizes our soul.
Sustains life.
All life.

326,000,000,000,000,000,000 = gallons of water on Earth (326 million trillion gallons).
75 percent of the Earth's surface is covered by water. Of that . . .
96.5 percent is salinated, undrinkable.
2 percent is frozen.
<1 percent is fresh, drinkable.

If we think of being thirsty, we are already dehydrated.
±50–60 percent = the amount of water in an adult human body.
±5–10 days = survive with no water.
±1 gallon of water = average daily consumption.
How much water did you drink today?
Was it pure? Was it filtered? From a bottle?

2017. 7,590,707,141 = world population.[4]
Annual world population growth = ±180 million people.
1 in 10 people lack access to safe water (±1 billion).

- - - - - - - - - - - - -

4   The data in this section can be accessed at worldometers.info, where the calculations are ongoing.

Water Consciousness

Women and children spend ±125 million hours each day collecting water.
More people have a mobile phone than a toilet.

The water crisis is the #1 global risk based on impact to society.[5]
2016. ±22 billion = the plastic water bottles in landfills or the environment.
2018. Water consumed this year 10,908,471,769 (million of liters).
2025. ±3 billion will face water-based vulnerability.
2050. ±9 billion is the forecast world population.

Water conservation. A luxury or a necessity?
You decide.

hope

---

5   For more information on this water crisis, go to water.org.

Water Consciousness

Water consciousness begins with us. The key is for our Eco-Conscious wisdom to stretch seamlessly around the world as a shared global commonality—to nourish our being while sustaining life of natural resources, especially water. As we consciously act on how, why, and when to use water, we unite as part of the solution and not the problem.

Do you remember the introductory thought in Chapter 1 inspiring me to write this book for you? It went like this: "As I watched the water swirl down the drain, I wondered how much water is wasted just from brushing teeth. I naturally turn off the water while brushing. Does everyone practice this ritual?"

A mini water quiz

- ❏ Do you consciously conserve water?
- ❏ As you turn the faucet to on, are you mindful of the flow?

Do you fill the bathtub to bathe . . .
- ❏ daily?
- ❏ to the top?

Do you have an ongoing drippy leak?
- ❏ Do you use gray water?
- ❏ Do you filter household water?
- ❏ Do you have your toolbox ready?

Are throwaway water bottles . . .
- ❏ in the refrigerator?
- ❏ on a counter?
- ❏ on a shelf?

- ❏ Are you ready to make changes to embrace water consciousness?

- ❏ Will you share your journey?
- ❏ Do you think beyond the toothbrush?

I encourage you to stand.
Walk, skip, hop, or run to the bathroom.
Take out your oral cleansing products.
Perform your teeth cleansing rhythmic routine.
Fini.

I ask . . . is this you?

The unconscious regimen
- ❏ Turn on the "H & C" tap water. The water is gushing!
- ❏ Apply the toothpaste. The water is still on.
- ❏ Brush teeth. Water continues to flow down the drain.
- ❏ Rinse. Still flowing.
- ❏ Floss. All that water.
- ❏ Swish mouthwash. Thirty seconds, one minute, the water is flowing.
- ❏ All of the above!

This is my pop-up bubble: Ugh!

Or . . . is this you?

The Eco-Conscious regimen
- ❏ Turn on the "C" tap water oh so slightly.
- ❏ Wet the toothbrush. Turn off the water.
- ❏ Apply toothpaste. The water is still off.
- ❏ Brush teeth. No water yet.
- ❏ Rinse. Add cold water to a small glass, sip, swish, spit. Repeat.
- ❏ Floss. Water is off.
- ❏ Swish an essential oil mouthwash. Swish with remaining glass of water, spit.
- ❏ All of the above!

This is my pop-up bubble: Yeah!

Eco-Reference Guide + Checklist—Water Considerations

Be Eco-Conscious, be purposeful, be empowered. Refer to this mini eco-key word reference guide while shopping for Tools of the Trade products. Add new favorites to your list. Your pathway to an Eco-Conscious, water-conscious healthy living lifestyle is well on its way.

Happy, Healthy Eco-Shopping!

Key Words (Enviro Benefits)	Our Future (online)	What It Means	Acronyms	Eco-Products
Conserve energy	5 Gyres Institute	Blackwater = unhealthy, unusable wastewater	± = approximately	
Conserve water	All About Water	Gray water = usable water from the sink, shower, bathtub	DPM = drips per month	
Crystals	Ban the Bottle	Low-flow = use less than 2.5 GPM	GPF = gallons per flush	
Energy efficient	Celebrate Toilet Day		GPM = gallons per minute	glass bottles

Water Consciousness

Green technology	Celebrate Water Day	GPY = gallons per year	low-flow toilets
High efficiency	Lenntech	HE = high efficiency	low-flow aerators
Low-flow	National Groundwater Awareness Week	HE = showerheads	solar tube lighting
Manufactured in an environmentally friendly way	Wakeup World		tankless water heater
Reduce your carbon footprint	World Water Day		
Support environmental sustainability			
Sustainable green product			

Innovative showerheads can save ±1 gallon of water per minute.

The time is now to let go . . . of unconscious water use!

The Approach

Eco-Conscious Water

You may wonder, Where do I begin? Which products are sustainable? Efficient? Of high performance? Do the gallons per flush (GPF) and gallons per minute (GPM) matter? Should the leaky faucet be a high-priority "fix-it" item on my to-do list? Is my showerhead model saving water? What is the quality of my water? Is the drinkable water quenching my thirst? Nourishing my well-being? Am I contributing to global pollution? What products are part of the solution to complement my aspiring Eco-Conscious Lifestyle?

Zealously, I share a treasure chest of Eco-Conscious water practices and PP products to guide you along your journey of transformation. As you read each mini section note your current concerns.

Create a "must-do" and "must-have" list.
Put each list into action.
Reap the rewards of those gratifying changes:
Releases impurities.
Renews your body.
Revitalizes your soul.
Sustains life.
All life.

The Bathroom

The overall intention is to use water-efficient products to preserve and protect our water supply. These products are innovative, reduce consumption, are of high performance and design, and nourish your well-being.

The Label

Knowledge = efficiency. While researching products—toilets, showerheads, tub fillers, faucets, filters, bottles, and accessories—look for credible, environmentally sustainable labels. When applicable, make reference to the GPF and GPM. The smaller the number, the less water usage. Do note: the WaterSense label is only extended to retailers independently certified who meet certain EPA criteria. Products bearing the Nordic Swan Ecolabel symbolize that stringent environmental criteria were met to achieve a sustainable society, to protect our Earth, resources, the consumer, and all life. Add new finds to your eco-reference guide.

What's In My Water

Each time you turn on the faucet, pour a glass of water, or step into the shower, the very essence of your being relishes the refreshing, high-quality, clear, sparkling, silky, tasty water. Otherwise, I ask, where is the motivation to begin a new day? With dirty, smelly, chemical-laden water?

To be free of undesirable, unhealthy impurities is vital. Test, filter, and retest your water. Before hiring an eco-professional or purchasing a filtration product, analyze the water with a basic informative online water diagnosis. Visit ecowater.com/waterresourcecenter/diagnose.

Note your "Diagnose My Water" results. Follow up with an eco-water pro to test your water. With a water quality report in hand, decide on the next step—to filter or not to filter the in-house water.

Water results + contact

Bathroom Filtration

Water filtration means a healthier you. Filtering household water enhances life and increases vitality. The gratifying benefits equate to water fresh from the spring. The type of system chosen depends on the impurities to remove followed by cost, size, design, and transportability. While researching options, look for the National Sanitation Foundation (NSF) Water Quality Certification to determine accurate performance.

Water filtration options:

bath faucet	glass water bottles	under counter
countertop	shower filters	whole home system

Product replacement filters and cartridges:
- Add replacement dates to your calendar.
- Set the recurring calendar alarm.
- Link-up—control and monitor via technology.

After considerable research, we chose a whole-house system to enrich the quality of the bathing and showering experience and regimens at the sink. For luxury-enhancing transportable convenience, I reach for a favored eco-chic glass water bottle. To refine the hydrating experience, the bottle of choice is infused with a gem pod and therapeutic essential oils to liven up and satisfy my thirst. Each sip is breathe-ably delicious and pure!

    PP: Whole house system and glass gemstone vial water bottle

Pencil in possibilities
Ink in absolutes

Throwaway Bottled Water

Disposable products are a global snag. Not all throwaway bottles are created equal. Throwaway water bottles are a growing phenomenon with a negative impact on our natural resources, our health, our flying feathered friends, and life within our waters.

Pollutes our Earth	Plastic bottles are not biodegradable. In North America alone, ±38 billion plastic bottles go to landfills, where they break down into teeny-tiny microplastic pieces leaching out harmful chemicals. And by the way, fish eat microplastics and we eat fish.
Harms the atmosphere	During manufacturing (life) and incineration (death), particulates enter the atmosphere creating pollution and impacting life (life after death).
Threatens global waters	Garbage patches are rapidly mounting in ocean gyres and seas. Impacts life. Takes life. Google for facts and unpleasant visuals.

Threatens marine life	The 5 Gyres Institute acknowledges, "More than 600 species are endangered or killed by marine plastic pollution."
Harmful to health	What's in your throwaway bottled water? Where was it mined? Tested? Did it receive exposure to heat during transportation and storage? It is leaching unwanted compounds into the water? Is it purer than your filtered tap water? Test your bottled water.

Set aside eight minutes to watch a short online movie called *The Story of Bottled Water*, presented by The Story of Stuff. It entertainingly explains the ugly truth about bottled water. After viewing and verbalizing at least nine gasping expressions, decide how you can be part of the solution to achieve sustainability.

PP: Story of Stuff

Eco-Bottle Etiquette

- A global remedy is needed.
- Ban the throwaway bottle.
- Make an influential, inspiring statement.
- Invest in eco-friendly reusable bottles.
- At home and in the office: drip several drops of a citrus pure essential oil into a glass or glass bottle of filtered water all day, every day. It's a staple.
- Power walks: same remedy, different eco-friendly bottle. Add a sleeve for protection.
- On the go—appointments, traveling, social engagements, shopping, and to-dos around town: same process, different bottle. Secure lid. Pop inside the ChaCha bag.
- Restaurants and entertainment: reach for a glass gemstone vial for a memorable experience.

All PP water bottles are sustainable, functional, aesthetically appealing, and liven up the taste to further promote an Eco-Conscious approach to a Healthy Living Lifestyle. Enjoy one sip at a time! Bye-bye, throw away water bottles.

PP: Glass bottles

My contribution, my pledge

Water Waste Sources

Wasting water in the bathroom is a breeze. A drippy, leaky toilet or faucet can waste hundreds to thousands of gallons of water per month. Letting water steadily flow from the faucet while performing other tasks is common and unmindful. How many gallons of water go to waste from the simple act of filling the bathtub? The amount is determined by the bathtub size and how often one bathes. With the average person flushing five times a day, toilets make up about 31 percent of overall household water consumption. Turn a knob, lift a handle, press a button, and let it flow. It's a repetitive act that requires no formal training. An inefficient showerhead and long showers account for approximately 17 percent water usage.

Let's use a scenario to put water waste into perspective.

Turn the shower on. As the cold water reaches the tile floor, it effortlessly travels down the drain. Once it warms to the ideal body temperature, you hop in—rinse down, lather up, rinse again, soap up, rinse again, shave, and perhaps brush those pearly whites. Fini? Not yet. The pulsating water feels so fab as it massages your body, you stay a little longer. Fini!

Identifying water waste sources is empowering and fun for the little ones, too. It's another step toward consciously conserving our natural water supply to support life—all life. It sets you on a purposeful journey to embrace mindful changes.

Identify

Filling a small bath to the tippy top =

±40–60 gallons of water!

How many gallons does it take to fill your bathtub?

_____

gallons

Eco-Reference Guide + Checklist—Water Waste Sources

Be Eco-Conscious, be purposeful, be empowered. Refer to this mini eco-key word reference guide to conserve water. Add new finds to your list. Your pathway to an Eco-Conscious, water conscious, healthy living lifestyle is well on its way.

Happy, Healthy Eco-Shopping!

At the Sink	In the Bathtub	In the Shower	In the Toilet Room
fast water flow	daily bathing	unplugging to drain hot water while adding cold water	broken flapper
filter screen: dirty mineral deposit	filling the bathtub	inefficient models	flushing after each yellow
inefficient products	inefficient models	low water pressure	flushing products other than toilet tissue
low water pressure	low water pressure	not capturing cold water in a container	flushing with clean drinkable water
water flows while multitasking	not plugging cold water as it heats up	water flows in the shower while multi-tasking in the shower	inefficient models

unconscious water running	water flows in the shower while multi-tasking outside the shower	inefficient products
unplugging to drain hot water while adding cold water		leaky toilet

Water Footprint Calculator

With a new awareness of water waste sources, approximate your daily water footprint. I took the test on February 15, 2017, to reveal daily water usage. Below is a cut, paste, and copy of the results.

Your water footprint:
1,229 Gallons/Day
Household: 2,502 Gallons/Day
The US Average is 2,220 Gallons/Day

PP: Google "water footprint calculator" or enter watercalculator.org

Water footprint

Tools of the Trade

It's time to gather Tools of the Trade products to minimize and/or eliminate water waste sources. The tools range from DIY gadgets to a low-flow toilet to filtration tools. Choose what is needed. No less. No more.

Eco-Conscious Water Solutions

Behind the Scene

What lurks behind the scene that no one else sees?

A drip
A tank
A cover
A light
A filter
?

Find the source: repair or replace. For instance, consider a tankless, on-demand water heater to conserve water. Insulate the hot water heater and water pipes to heat water quickly.

Reap the benefits of togetherness. Bring it all together. Choose DIY projects to Release, Renew, Revitalize. Have fun!

What's your story?

Drippy Leaks

Low water pressure indicates a possible leak. Gather a smartphone or pencil and paper. Read the water meter. Make certain no water flows from any source for over one hour. Reread the meter. If the reading changed, a leak is present. Find the source. To know how much that tiny leak is costing you daily and monthly, invest in a Drip Gauge, an inexpensive conservation tool.

At the Sink

Products	Consider WaterSense labeled faucets, aerators, and accessories for high performance and high efficiency.
DIY Products	◆ Install low-flow, high efficiency WaterSense labeled aerators to save water and reduce splash. ◆ Look for inexpensive, yet efficient 1.5 GPM, dual-threaded, and lead-free aerators. ◆ Remember to filter the water.
Eco-Consciousness	Turn the water off while brushing teeth, cleansing your face, washing hair, shaving, singing, and finding that "thing." A little bit goes a long way when it comes to washing hands morning, noon, night, and in-between. Consider applying a small squirt of waterless hand purifier to cleanse hands—no water required.

In the Bathtub

Products	Choose your bathtub collection wisely. Reference innovative technology, quality, ecology, and aesthetics. Consider WaterSense-labeled models for high performance and high efficiency. Water consciousness extends itself to smaller bathtub designs as well as lower GPM for a freestanding or deck-mount tub filler, tub spouts, and hand shower.
DIY Products	• Filter bath water to reduce the harmful effects of chlorine by approximately 90 percent in less than five minutes with a dechlorinating filter ball. Replace the filter after two hundred delightful bathing experiences. PP: Splish Splash Bath Filter
Eco-Consciousness	The bathing experience is a cleansing experience, regardless of age. So let's plug the hole as the water temperature warms. Fill partially, resisting the temptation to fill to the tippy top. Be mindful of how often you bathe, reserving for when special "me time" is calling. And remember the air you breathe should be breathe-ably delicious.

In the Shower

Products	Consider WaterSense-labeled showerheads for high performance and high efficiency. The lower the GPM (2.0, 1.6, 1.5), the more water saved. Shower-start technology exponentially reduces water waste with features such as built-in water temperature, pause settings, pause valve, and converters to reduce flow to a trickle. PP: Spoiler, EcoFlow, and Roadrunner are three favorites
DIY Products	• Measures the flow in GPM with a Shower Flow & Faucet Flow Meter Bag. • Reduce energy and water consumption with a smart water reader, an innovative monitoring device. The device shows—current water consumption, temperature, and energy efficiency class from A to G. Amphiro offers a1 basic and b1 connect (smartphone app). You choose. • Reduce shower time with a 5 Minute Shower Coach that suctions to the wall. Turn the water on and flip it. • Remove chlorine with a Premium Shower Filtration System and Cartridge. Replace the filter annually.
Eco-Consciousness	As the water warms to your delight, capture the cold water in a container to water plants, wipe the floor, and fill the toilet tank. Place a monitoring device inside the shower to keep you purposefully on track. Minimize the number of showers taken per day, shower younger children together, and shower in five minutes or less. All tasks beyond body washing assign to the sink regime—shaving, teeth brushing, face cleansing, and hair washing. Remember to clean the showerhead gasket often to prevent buildup.

The Toilet

Products	Replace older inefficient toilets with high performance and high efficiency models. Look for environmentally conscious products bearing the Swan Ecolabel and the WaterSense label. Consider dual-flush models—partial flush and full flush. The lower the GPF (1.28, 1.0, 0.9, 0.8, 0.5/0.95), the more water saved. Do note that compost toilet models are available that require no water for houses on and off the grid. To eliminate flapper repairs, consider a siphonic flush model or flapperless toilet. PP: Niagara Conservation, Toto, Kohler, EAGO Toilet, Biolet
DIY Products	• DIY tools are inexpensive. • Conserve additional water with each flush by placing a Toilet Tank Bank inside the tank. • To detect a leak, drop Leak Detection Tablets or food coloring dye inside the tank. If the water turns blue, the flapper is broken. When a leak is present install an Adjustable Toilet Flapper. • Save water with each flush with the Fill Master Fill Cycle Diverter. • Convert a standard flush toilet into a dual-flush with a HydroRight Drop-in Dual Flush Converter Kit. • Calculate the amount of water wasted from a leak with a Drip-Gauge Water measuring Vial. PP: AM Conservation Group and Eartheasy are two online favorites
Eco-Consciousness	Test for leaky drips. Add blue food dye inside the tank. Let the dye sit for an hour without flushing. If the water in the toilet bowl turns blue, a leak is present. Replace the broken flapper immediately. Save additional water with each flush: add gray water (used bath and shower water) to the tank. Simply scoop up a container of the water and pour into the toilet tank. As always, be conscious of what products are flushed down the toilet. Only flush toilet tissue and never flush toxic products, tampons, pads, paper towels, pills, or toys down the bowl. At appropriate times, remember this saying: When yellow, let it mellow.

The Professional

Certain projects require the expertise of a professional. Be prepared. Create an itemized list. Ask for a minimum of two referrals from a trusted source.

The professional & contact

AWARENESS ••• 297

The list

Little Things Make a Big Difference

In 1994, an aspiring scientist graciously gifted me a paperback book entitled *Proceedings of the Fifth National Conference, Water: Our Next Crisis?* I was hooked. From that day forward, a loyalty toward the importance of water quality, scarcity, and conservation flourishes.

You, too, can discover an array of water resources set forth by Eco-Conscious individuals, sustainable companies, organizations, committees, research centers, charitable groups, and more. Collectively they raise water-conscious awareness and propel to make change.

Consider a Google search titled water—awareness, quality, and conservation. With your new-found action-inspiring tools, you are well-equipped to make changes. Collectively it's the little things we do in our home, outdoors, and within our community that make a bigger difference. Simply ask yourself, "What's my niche?"

My hope is to actively raise water-conscious awareness and to be part of the solution.

Eco-Tips

- Join a local water research center to help preserve clean water.
- Learn of Always Water Smart on-line water conservation tips and tools.
- Download the EPA water sense checklist to save water.
- Take the on-line EPA water sense pledge (page 286).

Celebrate Annual Events

World Water Day (waterway.org)	March 22
World Toilet Day (toiletday.org)	November 19
SIWI World Water Week (worldwaterweek.org)	End of August and beginning of September
Global Handwashing Day (globalhandwashing.org)	October 15
National Groundwater Awareness Week (ngwa.org)	Second week of March

Values Learned

- Though I may, at times, be of unconscious mind, there is a message waiting to be revealed.
- Wasting water is of unconscious mind, while conserving water is of conscious mind.
- Water conservation is essential on all levels.
- Knowledge = Efficiency.
- I can be part of the solution.
- There is joy in sharing the truth about water to help achieve sustainability.

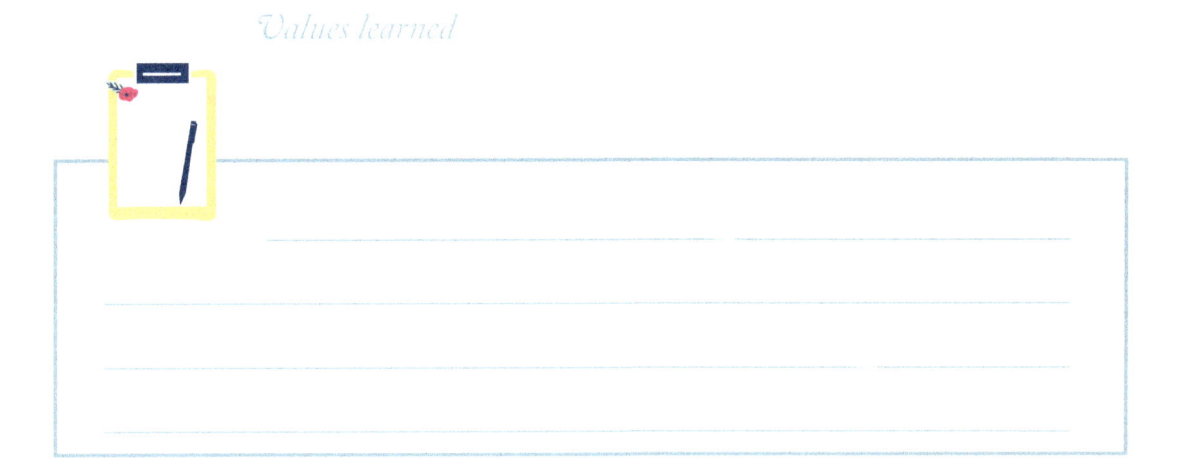

Values learned

Now I Know

- When I was a child, water was delivered to our home in glass bottles.
- My maternal grandfather piped a spring in the woods where I walked as a teenager.
- Water vulnerability is a thing.
- The smell and taste of plastic from throwaway water bottles was not a figment of my imagination.
- Throwaway bottled waters are a global snag.

Now I know

Your Story

Thoughts to Guide Your Thinking

- Water as a child . . .
- Color, odor, temperature . . .
- If only I knew . . .

Share water memories that flow with ease.

Pure Eco-Consciousness is flowing.
On to Chapter 9!

9

A Treasure Chest of Well-Being

MANIFEST

...There is only one thing
I ever work on with anyone, and this is
Loving the Self.

Love is the miracle cure.
Loving ourselves works miracles in our lives.

Love to me is appreciation
to such a degree that it fills my heart
to bursting and overflows.

—Louise L. Hay

My Story

The Birth of a Treasure Chest

My story is a reflection of inner passion to support the therapeutic benefits of nature's living energy, a journey that began long before my conscious mind recalls. Delve in and you will come to see the collection as timeless, holistic beauty rituals transforming a present state of well-being into pure bliss while fostering inner love and outer beauty.

As a preteen, I readily immersed myself in mini-beauty luxuries. The very thought of flickering candles and swirling steam while wrapped in cozy fluff lured me into the bathroom most often after sunset. Initial remedies were simple, basic. I cultivated a soothing environment to relax and infuse purity while releasing cares of the day. I was too young to realize the value of my in-home spa discovery.

As the years unfolded, I embraced the unveiling of self-awareness to encompass a lifestyle fostering holistic well-being, a lifestyle that came with ease and a stir of excitement. With customary familial guidance, I adopted heirloom remedies to nourish, beautify, heal, and uplift spirits. Each remain essential and are woven into my current lifestyle.

Interlacing mood enhancers with authentic treatments to pamper the senses became my personal signature style. For instance, today's beauty menu of delights offers a gradual transition into mind-body serenity. I commence with a pleasurable sage smudging ceremony to "Release" my body and the space of stagnant energies and to "Renew" with positive energy and well-being. The smudging is followed by a steady pulse of dry brushing to prep the skin for a natural glow. To "Revitalize," I mindfully slip into the warmth of an aromatic bath accompanied by the sensation of rhythmic facial tapping, gentle massaging, and splashes of a sweet body oil. Of course, the selection of mood enhancers sets the stage, blending seamlessly into the mini-spa retreat.

With ease, I present to you timeless recipes from my treasure chest of well-being. You will discover an assortment of favored beauty treatment ingredients to include gifts from our

Earth—organic fruits, vegetables, herbs, grains, and so forth. All deliver a plethora of benefits and are readily found in the kitchen, cupboards, and garden. I also include nine bona fide mood enhancers to support balance and harmony within you and in your haven.

Are you ready to create your own personalized, signature treasure chest and fill it with concoctions derived from natural organic substances that I love and trust?

My hope is for indulgence to prevail, bringing forth your inner light and outer glow.

Before You Begin

Create a treasure chest of well-being, a mini spa haven, in your sanctuary.

a.m.

noon

p.m.

sleep time

anytime

Prepare to	indulge in the pleasures of "me time" to Release, Renew, Revitalize your fantastical being.
Fill	your treasure chest with timeless, irresistibly simple recipes.
Identify	your awe-inspiring intention, a foundational motivating ingredient.
Listen to	inner intuition to select daily beauty rituals of posh delight.
Begin to	release clutter feelings while preparing the space.
Pamper	yourself in comfort, so cuddle up in comfy fluff.
Know	individual acts evolve into happy unified rituals.
Make way	for a self-designed menu to invoke self-love.

Treasure chest contents are arranged into four quadrants.

Mood Enhancers	Spa Essentials
spiritual	eco-tool kit
Eco-Tips	Beauty Rituals
guide	inspiring-action

Pure Eco-delight!

A Treasure Chest of Well-Being

This is only the beginning, for each juncture in life brings forth a new crystalized awareness to further elevate your Eco-Conscious approach to a beautiful Healthy Living Lifestyle.

love

Botanical-Infused Green Beauty Rituals

cleanse	de-puff	Release	beautify	cheer
exfoliate	stimulate	Renew	radiate	elevate
detoxify	circulate	Revitalize	glow	promote

and oh...so much more!

Mood Enhancers

Mood enhancers are a necessity to mindfully set the stage, to transform an everyday space into an inspiring haven, and to engage in breathe-ably delightful utopia experiences in your mini-spa haven.

A menu of mood enhancer essentials awaits. Each category provides an array of benefits to satisfy your senses and promote well-being. Choose each mood enhancer as you listen to your inner self for affirmation. Add selections to the Eco-Reference Guide + Checklist—Mood Enhancers.

Do note: personal favorites are mentioned as a guide.

Crystals + Gemstones

Choose the stone by letting the stone choose you. To heighten the experience, place a stone in a prominent area. Set an intention to manifest desires.
    PP:

amethyst = awareness	blue topaz = self-realization	green aventurine = manifest
angelite = communication	celestite = inner calm	lapis = truth
aquamarine = spiritual growth	citrine = happiness/ self-expression	rose quartz = unconditional love

Pink Himalayan Salt

Enhance the ambiance of the mini-spa setting with ancient gifts from the Himalayas while simultaneously releasing impurities and balancing the senses.

Glowing salt lamp	An array of designs await to suit the bathroom decor. Keep the lamp lit to release negative ions to improve IAQ and reap heath benefits, and to take delight in the warm, soft glow.
Salt wall	Custom-design an accent wall that releases negative ions— block, tile, or grain in an awe-inspiring pattern.

Salt-heart massage stones	Position two stones in a visible area. Gather to massage, cleanse, purify, and release negative ions. Use wet or dry, cool or warm.
Bath salts	Place fine or coarse salts in a decorative small bowl. Sprinkle salts into the bath along with several drops of an essential oil to Release, Renew, Revitalize.
Detox salt foot tiles	Warm in the oven and then place on the bathroom floor. Rest both feet on tile/blocks to pull out impurities.

Essential Oils

Add pure essential oils to beauty rituals. Splash in a bath. Spritz a towel. Diffuse the air. Manifest an intention. Consider mixing with a favored carrier oil before applying to the skin. Read the label. Suggested PPs are added to the timeless recipes. Check oils of interest. Be certain to include in your checklist.

PP:

calming	energizing	purifying	uplifting
❏ angelica	❏ bergamot	❏ eucalyptus	❏ bergamot
❏ chamomile	❏ cinnamon	❏ lemon	❏ ginger
❏ lavender	❏ clove	❏ lime	❏ jasmine
❏ tangerine	❏ peppermint	❏ orange	❏ myrrh
❏ rose	❏ rosemary	❏ peppermint	❏ grapefruit

balancing	passion	meditating	refreshing
❏ chamomile	❏ geranium	❏ frankincense	❏ grapefruit
❏ geranium	❏ jasmine	❏ myrrh	❏ lemon
❏ grapefruit	❏ ylang-ylang	❏ sandalwood	❏ lime
			❏ orange

Fragrant Botanicals

Awaken your senses with healthy, fresh, colorful delight inspired by nature.
- Burst of Sunshine Air Freshener
- Breezy Blossom Book Spray
- fresh flowers
- healthy plants
- white sage, loose-leaf

Lighting

Dim those lights for a soft-glow spa setting. Lighting options change with the seasons, time, decor, and mood. Simplify the options with a suitable dimmer switch.
- flickering
- glowing
- natural
- soft

   PP: Crystal Journey Candles

Music

Music soothes the soul and calms the mind. Be mindful of your selections.
- calming
- meditation

A Treasure Chest of Well-Being

- nature sounds
  PP: Andreas—Nature Angels

Beverage + Delights
Prepare a special area to place a beverage and small samplings of edible delights.
- reusable glass bottle—gempod
- cup of organic herbal luxury tea—white ginger pear
- filtered water—pure essential oils, fresh organic fruit
- fresh, organic fruit—melons, berries, oranges, kiwi
  PP: VitaJuwel Gem Vial and Tea Forte

ChaCha Bag
Be aware of free-flowing thoughts while relaxing in a green beauty ritual.
   Capture inspirations—writings, poetry, sketches—onto paper while fresh and alive.
- *A Timeless Keepsake*
- *pencil*

Enhance the ambiance with mood enhancers to mindfully engage in a mini-spa haven. Release, Renew, Revitalize!

Eco-Reference Guide + Checklist—Mood Enhancers

Prepare to set the stage. Create an eco-reference guide to reflect personal mood enhancer selections for present and future needs. Gather colored pencils to color code. Add new items to the list. Update changes.

Happy, Healthy Eco-Shopping!

Crystals + Gemstones	Pink Himalayan Salt	Essential Oils

Fragrant Botanicals	Lighting	Music	Beverage + Delights

Eco-Reference Guide + Checklist—Spa Essentials

With book in hand, walk to the bathroom closet, kitchen pantry, and garden to take inventory of essentials on hand. Note must-have items to purchase before a beauty ritual. Tweak ingredients to suit your style. Add personal favorites to the list.

Organic Products Please!

Fluff Essentials	Exfoliating Tools	Garden Tools
❏ comfy slippers	❏ bristle bath brush	❏ fresh floral petals
❏ facial cloth	❏ exfoliating washcloth	❏ small round stones
❏ fluffy socks	❏ hydro towel (must-have)	❏ herbs
❏ hair accessory	❏ long-handled skin brush (natural bristles)	❏ vegetables
❏ hand towels	❏ loofah brush	
❏ mitt	❏ shower gloves	
❏ pillows	❏ sponge	
❏ robe		
❏ spa moisture foot socks (overnight)		

A Treasure Chest of Well-Being

- ☐ spa moisture gloves (overnight)
- ☐ throw

Kitchen Tools

Utensils	**Pantry**	**Fridge Edibles**
☐ basin	☐ apple cider vinegar	☐ avocado
☐ bowl	☐ baking soda	☐ butter
☐ container	☐ carrier oils, liquid:	☐ cucumber
☐ decorative bottle	☐ avocado	☐ egg
☐ dipping bowl	☐ grapeseed	☐ lemon
☐ fork	☐ mixing	☐ milk
☐ glass dropper	☐ olive	☐ potato
☐ jar	☐ carrier oils, solid:	☐ mint leaves
☐ pot	☐ coconut oil (unrefined/raw)	☐ rosemary sprig

- ❏ steam
- ❏ water bottle
- ❏ whisk
- ❏ wooden spoon

- ❏ fractionated coconut oil
- ❏ unrefined shea butter
- ❏ unrefined coco butter lotion
- ❏ ground flaxseed
- ❏ herbal tea bags
- ❏ honey
- ❏ oatmeal
- ❏ Pink Himalayan Sea Salt
- ❏ sugar
- ❏ vitamin E soft gel

- ❏ sage
- ❏ unsweetened almond milk
- ❏ yogurt

Eco-Tips

- Select a special area for spa essentials—a drawer, shelf, basket, or cabinet. Give it a name.
- Specify bowls, basins, and socks for beauty rituals only.
- Spritz towels with Sweet Visions Linen Spray.
- When spontaneity strikes in, be ritual-ready.
- Tuck hair with an accessory.
- Begin each beauty ritual with freshly washed skin.
- Rinse that gorgeous face in an upward-and-out motion.
- Begin with tepid water to open pores.
- Finish with cold water to close pores.
- Do facial finger tapping to increase circulation and for a visible glow.
- Apply beauty facial rituals in a gentle circular, up and outward motion.
- Select the purest of ingredients (organic products please) to quench your in-the-moment "me time" needs. Enjoy samplings:

apple cider vinegar	soothes, tones, shines, cleanses
salt wall	hydrates, moisturizes, nourishes
carrier oil	moisturizes, repairs
cucumber	de-puffs, hydrates, refreshes, rejuvenates
egg white (oily skin)	shrinks pores, tightens, tones, hydrates, moisturizes
egg yolk (dry skin)	hydrates, nourishes, moisturizes
essential oil	purifies, beautifies
lemon	shrinks pores, tightens, tones, lightens
oatmeal	cleanses, exfoliates, soothes
raw honey	absorbs excess moisture, lightens, prevents

Charisse Marei's Timeless Eco-Beauty Recipes
Prepare in Advance

UPLIFTING BREATH

Gather

One 2-inch square decorative tile	3 drops pure essential oil (PP)

PREP
Place the sage on the nonporous decorative tile. To uplift spirits, drip drops of a mood-enhancing essential oil onto the small cluster of sage.

LET'S DO IT
Breathe in the mood-enhancing aromatics each time you visit the bathroom. Refresh as needed.
drip *lift *sniff

BODY LOVE SUGAR SCRUB

Gather

label	±15 drops of lavender, rosemary, or ylang ylang essential oil (PP)
lidded jar	1/4 cup liquid carrier oil (PP)
small bowl	1/2 cup raw brown sugar
spoon	1 tablespoon vegetable glycerine
	fresh rosemary sprig

PREP

Blend the first four ingredients in a bowl. Transfer to the jar. Add the sprig. Secure the lid. Adhere the label.

LIP LOVE SUGAR SCRUB

Gather

label	1 drop essential oil (PP)
lidded jar	2 teaspoons almond oil (PP)
small bowl	2 teaspoons local honey
spoon	1/4 cup raw brown sugar

The substitute . . . switch out the carrier oil for unrefined coconut oil.
The options . . . choose peppermint, orange, lime or any dietary essential oil.

PREP

Blend the ingredients in a bowl. Transfer to the jar. Secure the lid. Adhere the label.

*Enjoy each dip into the jar
and discover delight in each little leaf!*

Charisse Marei's Timeless Eco-Beauty Recipes + Rituals

MOUTH | RELEASE, RENEW, REVITALIZE

Beyond the Toothbrush—Vegan Style   time: 5-20 minutes

Gather

cotton round	±3 drops orange essential oil	mouth wash
natural silk floss	±3 teaspoons coconut oil (raw)	plant-based toothpaste
water flosser	apple cider vinegar	whitening tooth powder

LET'S DO IT

Oil Pulling	To rid mouth of toxins, swish coconut oil around gums and through teeth. Do not swallow. Spit oil into a tissue and discard into wastebasket. *swig * swish * spit*
Floss	Massage gums and remove food particles from hard-to-reach areas with a water flosser. *stream * glide * drip*

A Treasure Chest of Well-Being

Detox, Clean	Gently brush teeth and tongue with a delicious, all-natural toothpaste to detox, clean, polish, and brighten those pearly whites. Swish with an essential-oil mouthwash. *add * brush * spit*
Whiten, Brighten	Brighten teeth naturally with a whitening tooth powder. Be prepared, it's messy. *scoop * brush * spit*
Freshness	Drip drops of a pure dietary essential oil into a glass of water and the water bottle each time you fill up. *drip * swish * sip*
The Bonus	Multitask while swishing. Moisten a cotton round with vinegar. Dab face, neck, and clavicle (no eyes). Fan face or add bits of water to soothe the tingle. *wet * dab * fan*

Flavor each breath, thought, and step with zing!

EYES + LIPS | RELEASE, RENEW, REVITALIZE

Eye De-Puff   time: PP

Gather

dipping bowl	2 herbal tea bags	facial cloth
water		hand towel
		linen spray

The substitute . . . two cucumber slices.
Multitask . . . combine with a foot soak.

PREP
Heat water. Steep those tea bags till plump. Transfer into a small bowl and cover with the facial cloth. Moisten towel in tepid water and spritz with spray. Roll to maintain heat.

LET'S DO IT
Gently squish tea bags to release excess water. Position yourself on those fluffy pillows and get comfy. Place warm bags over those puffy eyes and gently lie warm towel over face. Rest and manifest uplifting thoughts. Finish up with a dab of nourishing eye cream. Apply with ring finger from the outside corner in.
dip * do * drip

Lip Retreat

time: before sleep

Gather

Lip Love Sugar Scrub   facial cloth

PREP
Open the jar and prepare to slough off dry skin, increase circulation, and to promote healthier silky-smooth lips.

LET'S DO IT
Scoop a small amount from the jar. With a light touch, exfoliate in a circular motion. Rinse with cool water. Pat dry. Nourish those lips with vitamin E.
*scrub * rinse * dab*

Eye Suppleness

time: before sleep

Gather

One natural vitamin E softgel

PREP
Bedtime eyes. Cleanse face and hands. Pat dry. Nip the tip off the softgel capsule. Squeeze onto ring finger. Pat two ring fingers together.

LET'S DO IT
Gently dab vitamin E around the entire eye to enhance suppleness. Start at the outer corner and dab inward. Saturate those luscious lips, too.
*nip * dab * go*

*Love, live, laugh
with intention!*

FACE | RELEASE, RENEW, REVITALIZE

The Plug-In Facial Steam   time: PP

Gather

facial steam plug-in	Pink Himalayan Sea Salt	hair accessory
	water	hand towel

PREP
Add water and salt to the steamer. Securely position hair accessory. Cleanse areas to pamper with an *au naturel* wash.

LET'S DO IT
Lower face a comfortable distance over the burbling steamer. Drape the towel over head to maintain steam and increase sweat. With eyes closed, visualize your pores opening and impurities releasing. When finished follow with ten quick splashes of cold water to close pores, or pat dry with the hand towel (no splashes) and continue with a facial mask.
*add * drape * go*

The Bowl Facial Steam time: PP

Gather

bowl	±3 drops essential oil (PP)	facial cloth
pot	fresh flower petals	hair accessory
	water	hand towel
		linen spray

PREP
Securely position hair accessory. Cleanse areas to pamper with an *au naturel* wash. Boil water and transfer to a bowl. Add essential oil and flower petals.

LET'S DO IT
Lower face a comfortable distance over bowl. Drape the towel over head to maintain steam and increase sweat. With eyes closed, visualize your pores opening and impurities releasing. Follow with ten quick splashes of cold water to close pores. Pat dry and continue with a facial mask.
*add * drape * go*

Live with joyful, colorful emotion!

Eco-Facial Mask—The Egg   time: PP

Gather

bowl	organic egg	facial mitt/cloth
makeup brush	vitamin E softgel	hair accessory
whisk	water	hand towel
		linen spray

PREP
Prepare to tighten and tone for gorgeous glowing skin. Choose the egg white or yolk. Cleanse areas to pamper—face, neck, clavicle—with an *au naturel* wash. Drape and tuck towel to protect top from unexpected splashes.

Whipped White Mask	Tap the egg on the rim of the bowl. Separate the white into the bowl, discard the yolk. Whisk to a fluffy frothy texture. Apply with fingers.
Whipped Yolk Mask	Tap the egg on the rim of the bowl. Separate the yolk into the bowl, discard the white. Whisk. Apply with brush.

LET'S DO IT
Nourish eyes with a dab of vitamin E. Swoosh up egg mixture with fingers or brush to gently dab and layer on. Position yourself on those fluffy pillows and get comfy. As the mask tightens, relax facial muscles, tongue, neck, and shoulders. Remove with tepid water and mitt. Follow with ten splashes of icy cold water to close pores. Pat dry. Moisturize.
add* dab* pat

The Eggless Egg—Vegan Style time: PP

Gather

bowl	1 tablespoon ground flaxseed	facial mitt/cloth
makeup brush	1 tablespoon honey	hair accessory
whisk	2 tablespoons water	hand towel
	vitamin E softgel	linen spray

PREP
Prepare to exfoliate, tighten, and tone for gorgeous glowing skin. Combine flaxseed, water, and honey in a small bowl. Let sit for ten-ish minutes for egg-like, non-drippy consistency. In the meantime, cleanse areas to pamper with an *au naturel* wash. Drape and tuck towel to protect top from unexpected splashes.

LET'S DO IT
Nourish eyes with a dab of vitamin E. Swoosh up mixture with fingers and dab on face, neck, and clavicle. Be prepared to include arms and hands with extra mixture. Multitask with squats or position yourself on those fluffy pillows and get comfy. Enjoy your special time. Remove with tepid water and mitt. Hop in the shower or follow with ten splashes of icy cold water to close pores. Pat dry. Moisturize.

add* dab* pat

You
A glass of pure water
2 drops of a citrusy essential oil
stir + sip = ahh!

The Avocado, the Cucumber, and the . . .   time: PP

Gather

special dish	avocado	facial cloth
masher	1/4 cup uncooked oatmeal	hair accessory
	2 tablespoons local raw honey	2 hand towels
	2 slices cucumber	linen spray

The bonus . . . avocado seed ball and drops of lime essential oil.

PREP
Securely position hair accessory. Cleanse areas to pamper with an *au naturel* wash. Place the hand towel on the vanity and position the dish on top. Protect clothing with a drape and tuck of the towel. Remove the avocado's outer skin and ball seed. Save the ball. Mash the fleshy part into a creamy paste. Add the oatmeal and honey. Keep extra mixture in dish.

LET'S DO IT
Scoop up small portions with your fingertips and dab around face, neck, and clavicle. Yep! Include those luscious lips, too. Place the hand towel over the pillow.

Quiet "Me Time"	:	Position yourself on those fluffy pillows and get comfy. Rhythmically plop a cucumber over each eye and gracefully drift away. Relax and enjoy some music.
Massage & Rinse Time	:	Divide the remaining mixture into four sections. Scoop up to exfoliate and massage one foot at a time. Add a few drops of lime essential oil to the mixture in hand. With retained avocado ball, massage with hands and ball—under, over, and between those toes. Rinse feet in the sink or shower. Repeat the steps applying to hands and forearms. Rinse time, face, too. Ahh! Fresh and invigorated for hours to come. Pat dry. Moisturize.

*add * dab * go*

THE NO-DRIP RECIPE

The Honey, the Oats, and the . . .   time: PP

Gather

special dish	2 tablespoons local raw honey	facial cloth
	1/4 cup uncooked oatmeal	hair accessory
	2 teaspoons lemon juice	2 hand towels
	vitamin E softgel	linen spray

The bonus. Avocado seed ball and drops of lime essential oil.

PREP
Securely position hair accessory. Cleanse areas to pamper with an *au naturel* wash. Place the hand towel on the vanity and position the dish on top. Protect clothing with a drape and tuck of the towel. Add honey, oats, and lemon juice to the dish.

LET'S DO IT
Nourish eyes with a dab of vitamin E. Blend dish ingredients together with fingertips. Scoop up small portions. Apply tiny rhythmic circular movements over face, neck, and clavicle. Layer and dab to your hearts content. Yep! Include those luscious lips, too. Keep extra mixture in dish.

Multitask	This non-drippy texture allows you the opportunity to reap the essential mask benefits while performing other tasks.
Massage & Rinse Time	Divide the remaining mixture into four sections. Scoop up to exfoliate and massage one foot at a time. Add a few drops of lime essential oil to the mixture in hand. Massage with hands and retained avocado ball—under, over, and between those toes. Rinse feet in the sink or shower. Repeat the steps and apply to hands and forearms. Rinse time, face, too. Ahh! Fresh and invigorated for hours to come. Pat dry. Moisturize.

*add * dab * go*

You
Let the creativity flow!
Move, wiggle, dance, sing!

A Treasure Chest of Well-Being

HAIR | RELEASE, RENEW, REVITALIZE

The Hair Mask   time: ± 20 minutes

Gather

mini whisk	5 drops jasmine essential oil	hand towel
small bowl	2 teaspoons Asian Pear Blossom Honey	mitt
	2 organic egg yolks	

The bonus . . . avocado flesh.

PREP
Tap the egg on the rim of the bowl. Separate the yolk into the bowl, discard the white. Rhythmically whisk yolk, honey, and oil until blended.

LET'S DO IT
Scoop up small portions and smooth over the scalp. Revitalize. Apply a gentle massage.
add * *glide* * *ahh*

Multitask. Get messy with the remaining mixture. Smooth a thin layer over face, neck, clavicle, and arms. Massage or finger-tap to promote circulation. Rinse hair and body in the shower.

HANDS + FEET | RELEASE, RENEW, REVITALIZE

The Foot Soak   time: PP

Gather

basin	±4 drops peppermint essential oil	cotton foot socks
bath mat	carrier oil	fluffy throw
bowl (optional)	fresh flower petals	hand towels
journal	fresh mint leaves	linen spray
stones	tepid water	

The substitute . . . switch out the foot soak for a revitalizing hand soak. Add ingredients to a pretty bowl.

The bonus . . . pull up a fluffy bath rug for your furry friend to soak up the aromatic delights, too!

PREP
Cleanse areas to pamper with an *au naturel* wash. Position basin on top of a bath mat. Add stones, water, and drops of essential oil. Place essentials within arm's reach—leaves, petals, beverage, journal, throw.

LET'S DO IT
Position yourself with those fluffy pillows to get comfy. Dip your toes into the water. As you set an intention, mindfully top the water with mint leaves and flower petals. Allow your being to embrace the moment. Breathe. Transfer thoughts of enlightenment into your journal. Your intuition will guide you to the next phase.

Gently pat each foot dry with the scented hand towel.

A Treasure Chest of Well-Being

Blend, in the palm of your hand, a dab of essential oil (PP) with a few drops of a favored carrier oil. Massage the underside and tops of feet, ankles, and calves with fingertips and thumbs. Wrap feet together in the warm scented towel. Prop up, sit back, and enjoy the pleasures of a bit more tranquility. Then slip those gorgeous feet into a pair of fluffy socks or a pair of sneakers and go for it.

add* dip* wrap

Or ditch the socks and continue with a body polish scrub.

The Body Scrub   time: before sleep

Gather

Body Love Sugar Scrub   :   hand towel   :   body cream

PREP
Prepare to slough away dryness and increase circulation for healthier silky-smooth skin. Exfoliate out of the shower on a non-slid surface. Whether to so stand, sit, or prop legs is determined by flexibility, stability, and age.

LET'S DO IT
Moisten skin with tepid water. Spoon dabs of scrub onto your palms. Gently massage in tiny circular motions (no face). Rinse. Pat dry. Moisturize. Continue with Beauty Ritual: *The Foot Massage.*

The Foot Massage   time: PP

Gather

aroma stone (tourmaline stones)	carrier oil (PP)	spa moisture cotton foot socks
journal	essential oil (PP)	spa moisture cotton gloves

PREP
Choose a comfy place to sit and position the sauna accordingly. Add drops of an essential oil to the divets (tourmaline stones).

LET'S DO IT
Fluff those pillows and get comfy. Enjoy the aromatics and well-needed foot massage. This is your "me time" to meditate and journal inspirations. Afterward, pamper those loyal hands and feet with an additional touch of nourishment. Blend an ample amount of carrier oil (PP) and drops of essential oil (PP) onto your palm. Massage into skin with gentle rhythmic motions. Slip on the foot socks and then gloves. Remove in the morning.

*add * massage * wrap*

The Foot Detox   time: ± 10 minutes/daily

Gather

diffuser

Himalayan Salt Detox Foot Tiles/Blocks

journal

pencil

beverage

essential oil (PP)

PREP
Warm up the foot tiles for heat therapy or refrigerate for cold therapy. Add drops of an essential oil to the diffuser or to your wrist. Choose a comfy place to sit. Position the tiles on the floor in front of the seat.

LET'S DO IT
Fluff those pillows and get comfy. Place feet on the tiles to naturally release impurities. Breathe in the aromatics to soothe and rejuvenate your being. This is your "me time" to meditate or journal inspirations.
*prep * place * wipe*

You
A glass of pure water
3 drops of orange essential oil
stir, sip, sip
ahh!

BODY | RELEASE, RENEW, REVITALIZE

The Sauna   time: PP

Gather

infrared sauna	beverage	linen spray
journal	essential oil (PP)	fluffy towels
pencil		

The bonus . . . a pair of Himalayan Salt Detox Foot Tiles/Blocks for added spa therapy.

PREP
Prepare to release unwanted toxins through your sweat glands. Cleanse with an *au naturel* wash to remove body lotion. Slip into a fluffy robe or towel and tuck hair in a hair wrap. Place foot tiles on the floor. Add a few drops of an essential oil to the aroma cup. No cup? Spritz away.

LET'S DO IT
Position feet on the tiles (optional) and get comfy. Allow the cares of the day to melt away with each aromatic breath. Meditate or journal inspirations.
wrap * drip * sip

Dry Brushing   time: daily routine

Gather

One natural fiber skin brush (long-handle) with cactus bristles

body cream

PREP
Prepare to slough, boost, stimulate, detox, smooth, and energize. Remove garb. Have dry brush ready.

LET'S DO IT
Dry brush before showering. Brush with gentle, long upward strokes and small circular motions toward your heart. Start at the underside of your feet up each leg, from the tips of your fingers up each arm, back, and front torso. Shower. Buff dry. Moisturize.
shed buff* glow*

The Shower   time: 5 minutes

Gather

| body wash | essential oil (PP) | hydro towel |
| exfoliating tool | body cream | fluffy towels |

PREP
Gather products and place in the shower.

LET'S DO IT
Slip on exfoliating gloves or reach for the towel and suds up. As the topical cleaning takes place consciously release clutter feelings lingering within. Allow the grime to swirl down the drain. Breathe in the essential oil aromatics to uplift and soothe your mind, body, and soul. Manifest joyful thoughts.
*suds * shed * glow*

Hard-to-reach areas. Add bath gel to the exfoliating towel. Rub together to create lather. Open to hold both ends of the towel.

Back and derriere. Position towel behind shoulders. Apply gentle side-to-side and top-to-bottom angular movements.

Feet. Position the towel under one foot. Stand or sit to steadily exfoliate with side-to-side motions.

Finish up with a cool rinse. Pat dry. Moisturize.

The Soak

time: PP

Gather

bath caddy	±8 drops pure essential oil (PP)	bathing pillow
decorative bowl	beverage	fluffy towels
Himalayan fine grain bath salts	fresh flower petals	

PREP
Select a calming, relaxing, or loving essential oil to pamper in luxury. Add drops of the oil and bath salts to a bowl and swish. Sprinkle the blend into the bath water. Swish to evenly distribute and dissolve. Gently toss fragrant flower petals into the bath water—gardenia, rose, jasmine, magnolia. Place accessories and a favorite beverage on the bath caddy and position in the tub. Play beautiful inspirational music to soothe your being. Prepare to immerse in the warmth of the velvety water to soothe the body and relax the mind while uplifting spirits.

LET'S DO IT
Dip into the water and gently lie back to rest on the pillow. Slip into a mindful place of serenity. Intermittently, sip from the warmth of the cup or enjoy the crisp delight of a cool beverage. Just breathe.

add * *swish* * *sip*

You
"Me time"
One soothing bath
Six drops of jasmine essential oil
relax, soak, breathe!

Values Learned

- Life is a treasure chest of the known and of exploration.
- Botanical recipes nourish the soul, mind, body, and aura.
- To be grateful is the seed and the seed within the seed.
- Live with joyful, colorful emotion.

Values learned

Now I Know

- Self-designed menus are a reflection of my personal style story.
- Mood enhancers are essential to invoke pure delight.
- Flavor each breath, thought, and step with zing.
- Capture inspirations while fresh and alive.

Now I know

Your Story

Thoughts to Guide Your Thinking

- Timeless holistic beauty rituals ...
- Authentic treatments to pamper the senses ...
- Bring forth your inner light and outer glow ...

When was the birth of my treasure chest?

Your aura radiates in full splendor.
On to Chapter 10!

10

PP Eco-Resources

LOVE .....

You are what you are and where you are
because of what has gone into your mind.

You can change
what you are and where you are
by changing what goes into your mind.

– Zig Ziglar

Welcome to the personalized mini chapter of eco-resources. It is designed for your organizational delight and to provide ease while simultaneously saving valuable research time. Do note that this is only a sampling.

When you connect with me on social media, in person, and at the *Charisse Marei* website, you will discover a host of additional eco-brands I love. You will also meet "The Girls,"—Sage, aka "Princess Lilly," and Citrus, my lovable one-eyed puppy.

Happy, Healthy Exploring + Shopping!

Online Shopping

Dyson
www.dyson.com
Efficient home products

Jeffrey Court
www.jeffreycourt.com
Decorative tile

Interior Design Tools
www.interiordesigntools.com
Space planning system

Caboo
www.cabooproducts.com
Ecologically sustainable paper products

Online Eco Groups + Organizations

AM Conservation Group
www.amconservationgroup.com
Energy and water efficient products

Grace Communications Foundation
www.gracelinks.org
Supports our Earth

Beyond Pesticides
www.beyondpesticides.org
Protecting health + environment

Story of Stuff
www.storyofstuff.org
Refining consumer choices

Earth Day Network
www.earthday.org
Worldwide environmental movement

Water
www.water.org
How to end the water crisis

Quoted Authors

The Hidden Messages in Water
by Masaru Emoto

Speech by Gandhi, Kingsley Hall, London 17 October 1931
by Mahatma Gandhi

The Greatest Miracle in the World
by Og Mandino

You Can Heal Your Life
by Louise L. Hay

Organic Manifesto: How Organic Farming Can Heal Our Planet, Feed the World, and Keep Us Safe
by Maria Rodale

Other Like-Minded Earth-Friendly Authors

Your Spacious Self: clear the clutter and discover who you are
by Stephanie Bennett Vogt

Gorgeously Green: 8 Simple Steps to An Earth-Friendly Life
by Sophie Uliano

A Child's Introduction To The Environment
by Michael Driscoll & Professor Dennis Driscoll

Earthing: The most important health discovery ever?
by Clinton Ober, Stephen T. Sinatra, M.D., Martin Zucker

The Natural House Book: Creating A Healthy, Harmonious, and Ecologically Sound Home Environment
by David Pearson

TheoSophia's Wisdom School
by TheoSophia Rose

Other Authors That I Love

Callanetics for Your Back
by Callan Pickney

Is It True They Call You The Dog Bed Fairy?
by Shannon McLinden

Paris: Through A Fashion Eye
by Megan Hess

French Women Don't Get Fat
by Mirelle Guiliano

The One Gift
by D. Gary Young

The Woman's Book of Courage
by Sue Patton Thoele

Charisse Marei is the modern day representation of the Eco-Conscious home and beautiful living. My signature: you don't have to spend a lot of money to have your home breathe-able, beautiful, and eco-chic. Stay informed of updates—upcoming and newly released books, products, printables, and programs designed to Revitalize (3Rs) yourself, home, furry friends, and our Earth. It's sure to be an empowering journey of inspiration and transformation.

Come with us. Join our eco-team. Help spread eco-ness!

Release

Revitalize

Renew

www.CharisseMarei.com

To submit a book review:
www.CHARISSEMAREI.com/bookreview

Follow *Charisse Marei* on social media to receive inspirational Eco-Conscious, Healthy-Living Lifestyle messages:
facebook.com/CharisseMarei
twitter.com/CharisseMarei
instagram.com/CharisseMarei

My hope is for you to join our team to live, eat, and breathe the most beautiful Eco-Conscious, Healthy-Living Lifestyle imaginable and then share your gift with others.

Acknowledgments

Who would have imagined that a young mother of three (me) who struggled to write a one-page paper in college would become a published author? I certainly have angels on my shoulders.

With heartfelt passion, I wish to acknowledge the beautiful people who recognized the sleeping author within and to those that gave encouragement and support to write this book.

To Professor Christian Kulczytzky: With sheer genuineness in recognition of my writings, you planted an, "I believe in you" seed. Blessings to you for seeing what I had yet to see.

To Christina Leeson: A visionary light, for awakening my purpose as an instrument to write, inspire, and guide.

To my husband and friend, Dr. Drew Ronnermann: You gave unconditional, loving support every step of the way. Your cute gesture of showering me with bunches of fresh flowers brought joy to my being and a touch of vibrant energy to our home.

There is only one happiness in life, to love and be loved. —George Sand

To my parents and siblings: You are my be-all foundation, support system, my today and future. Love always.

To my children and grand children: You journey in my conscious footsteps; thank you for your encouragement and love. You are my breath.

To my dear friends: Your gracious support adds a spark of uplifting energy when most needed. An extra special note of appreciation to Dr. Michele Shade for collaborating on the creation of the ChaCha Bracelet. Our gathering on Sunday afternoons around the kitchen table with Lisa, Tammy, and Leah to produce the first 100 bracelets and to enjoy edible delights is a forever gift of joy.

To Joshua, Sammy, Sarah and my design and publishing team at Friesen Press: I am delighted our paths met. You simplified the process of bookmaking while transforming my vision into reality. Blessings to each of you.

To Candace: I am forever grateful to you and your company—Change it Up Editing and Writing Services. Your ongoing guidance and quick turnaround time means the world to me.

To Reni and the design team at Bliss and Tell Branding: You effortlessly bring joy to my being. The branding and website are simply gorgeous!

To you, my delightful readers, thank you for your support and for seeking a journey along an eco-conscious path of discovery to fulfill a greater purpose. Love this book as though it were your velveteen rabbit.

To all the special people who worked diligently behind the scene to help bring my vision to light: I am thankful for you always.

My heart sings to you.

About the Author

Charisse Marei is an eco-conscious interior designer and "authorpreneur" who empowers and inspires people from all walks of life. As a passionate advocate for a healthy, eco-living lifestyle, she focusses on transforming interiors into beautiful, breathe-able dwellings combining her formal training in building biology, green design, feng shui, and essential oils with her passion for infusing harmony and balance, inspiration and purpose.

She is a graduate of Philadelphia College of Textile & Science and the International Institute for Building-Biology & Ecology, and had careers in interior and aviation design before launching her successful boutique design consultancy. She is the visionary, creative director, and illustrator of her work, including two books: *The Bathroom*, the first book in the series One Room at a Time: Your Essential Guide to an Eco-Conscious, Healthy-Living Lifestyle, and *A Timeless Keepsake*. She is the creator of the ChaCha and the ChaCha Mini Gem bracelets, designed to unify and empower women around the world, and of the lifestyle website **Charisse Marei**.

Her home is nestled in the beautiful rolling hills of Pennsylvania, where she lives with her husband, Dr. Drew, and "The Girls," Sage and Citrus, their two Bichons Frise. She is a daughter, sister, mother, and ChaCha to her seven grandchildren.

Her best days are spent working in her studio alongside "The Girls."

Learn more at charissemarei.com

This is only the beginning!

◆ FriesenPress

Suite 300 - 990 Fort St
Victoria, BC, V8V 3K2
Canada

www.friesenpress.com

Copyright © 2018 by Charisse Marei
First Edition — 2018

Illustrated by Charisse Marei and Bliss & Tell

All rights reserved.

The information presented in The Bathroom is for informational value only and is designed to help you make informed decisions about your home and lifestyle. Neither the author nor publisher takes responsibility, expressed or implied, for any adverse effects or consequences resulting from the use of any of the suggestions, preparations, or procedures from reading or following the information in this book. Always follow manufacturer instructions for application, care, and cleaning. Always test a formula before application. Keep all suggested products in a safe place out of reach of children and pets.

No part of this publication may be reproduced in any form, or by any means, electronic or mechanical, including photocopying, recording, or any information browsing, storage, or retrieval system, without permission in writing from FriesenPress.

ISBN
978-1-5255-2060-0 (Hardcover)
978-1-5255-2061-7 (Paperback)
978-1-5255-2062-4 (eBook)

1. HOUSE & HOME

Distributed to the trade by The Ingram Book Company

CPSIA information can be obtained
at www.ICGtesting.com
Printed in the USA
BVOW05s2250110218
507847BV00004B/8/P